Adobe®
Encore™ DVD

Classroom in a Book®

Adobe

www.adobepress.com

Contents

Lesson 03   ## Designing Menus in Adobe Photoshop

Lesson 04   ## Using Adobe Encore DVD Templates

Getting Started

Adobe® Encore™ DVD gives you the tools you need to let you effortlessly create and burn customized DVDs. You can design menus and buttons in Adobe Encore DVD, or use menus and buttons you create in Adobe® Photoshop®. The navigational tools in Adobe Encore DVD give you total control over the viewers' experience of your DVD. Whether you're a corporate communications professional or an aspiring videographer, you'll enjoy the versatility, ease of use, and power of Adobe Encore DVD software.

About Classroom in a Book

Adobe Encore DVD Classroom in a Book® is part of the official training series for Adobe graphics and publishing software developed with the help of experts at Adobe Systems. The lessons are designed to let you learn at your own pace.

Although each lesson provides step-by-step instructions for creating a specific project, there's room for exploration and experimentation. You can follow the book from start to finish or do only the lessons that correspond to your interests and needs.

Prerequisites

Before beginning to use *Adobe Encore DVD Classroom in a Book*, you should have a working knowledge of your computer and the Windows operating system. Make sure that you know how to use the mouse and standard menus and commands and that you know how to open, save, and close files. If you need to review these techniques, see the printed or online documentation included with your Windows operating system. It is also helpful, but not necessary, to have experience with Adobe Photoshop, Adobe® Premiere®, and Adobe® After Effects®.

To complete some of the projects, you will need to have Adobe Photoshop, Adobe Premiere Pro, or Adobe After Effects installed on your system.

Note: You can use either Adobe Photoshop 7.0 or Adobe Photoshop CS with Adobe Encore DVD. Where necessary, instructions for each version of Photoshop are written separately.

Installing the Adobe Encore DVD program

Before you begin using *Adobe Encore DVD Classroom in a Book*, make sure that your system is set up correctly and that you've installed the required software and hardware. You must purchase the Adobe Encore DVD software separately. For system requirements and complete instructions on installing the software, see the documentation included with your Adobe Encore DVD application DVD.

You must install the application from the Adobe Encore DVD application DVD onto your hard disk; you cannot run the program directly from the DVD-ROM. Follow the on-screen instructions. Make sure the serial number for your Adobe Encore DVD software is accessible before installing the application; you can find the serial number on the back of the DVD case.

Starting Adobe Encore DVD

You start Adobe Encore DVD just as you would any software application. In Windows, choose Start > Programs > Adobe Encore DVD 1.0.

Installing the fonts you'll use in Classroom in a Book projects

The fonts used in the lessons in this book are included on the Adobe Encore DVD application DVD. Ensure that the fonts are available before you begin working with the lessons. If the fonts are not installed on your system, install them from the Adobe Encore DVD DVD-ROM, following the on-screen instructions.

Copying the Classroom in a Book files

The *Adobe Encore DVD Classroom in a Book* DVD includes folders containing all the electronic files for the lessons. Each lesson has its own folder, and you must copy the folders to your hard drive to do the lessons. To save room on your drive, you can install only the folder for each lesson as you need it, and remove the folder when you're done.

To install the Classroom in a Book files:

1 Insert the *Adobe Encore DVD Classroom in a Book* DVD into your DVD-ROM drive.

2 Create a folder named Encore_CIB on your hard drive.

3 Copy the lessons you want to your hard drive:

• To copy all the lessons, drag the Lessons folder from the DVD into the Encore_CIB folder.

• To copy a single lesson, drag the individual lesson folder from the DVD into the Encore_CIB folder.

Note: As you work through each lesson, you may overwrite the original files. To restore the original files, recopy the corresponding lesson folder from the Classroom in a Book DVD to the Encore_CIB folder on your hard drive.

Additional resources

Adobe Encore DVD Classroom in a Book is not intended to replace documentation that comes with the Adobe Encore DVD program. Only the commands and options used in the lessons are explained in this book. For comprehensive information about program features, refer to these resources:

• *The Adobe Encore DVD User Guide*, which is included with the Adobe Encore DVD software, contains a complete description of all features in the software.

• Online Help, an online version of the user guide, is accessible by choosing Help > Contents from the Adobe Encore DVD title bar.

• The Adobe Web site (www.adobe.com) can be viewed by choosing Help > Adobe Online if you have a connection to the World Wide Web.

Adobe Certification

The Adobe Training and Certification Programs are designed to help Adobe customers improve and promote their product-proficiency skills. The Adobe Certified Expert (ACE) program is designed to recognize the high-level skills of expert users. Adobe Certified Training Providers (ACTP) use only Adobe Certified Experts to teach Adobe software classes. Available in either ACTP classrooms or on-site, the ACE program is the best way to master Adobe products. For Adobe Certified Training Programs information, visit the Partnering with Adobe Web site at http://partners.adobe.com.

Lesson 1

1 Creating a Simple DVD

A DVD project includes video files, audio files, and menus. With Adobe Encore DVD, you can easily put the pieces together to create a simple DVD. In this lesson, you'll learn about the core tools in Adobe Encore DVD as you create a project from start to finish.

This lesson introduces the Adobe Encore DVD workspace and basic concepts. In it, you will learn how to do the following:

- Create a new project.

- Import files as assets.

- Import a layered Adobe Photoshop file as a menu.

- Create chapter points.

- Link buttons on a menu to chapter points.

- Set start and end behaviors.

- Set menu and title behaviors.

- Preview a DVD project.

- Burn a DVD.

Getting started

In this lesson, you'll create an Adobe Encore DVD project from start to finish. You'll create a new project, import the assets and menu for the project, create links and behaviors, preview the DVD, and burn the DVD. Make sure you know the location of the file you need for Lesson 1. For help, see "Copying the Classroom in a Book files" on page 2.

Viewing the finished Adobe Encore DVD project

To see what you'll be creating, take a look at the finished project.

1 Start Adobe Encore DVD.

2 Choose File > Open Project.

3 In the Open dialog box, navigate to the Lesson 01 folder. Select **Lesson_01_end.ncor**, and then click Open.

The Adobe Encore DVD workspace opens. By default, only some of the windows shown below are open. The Project window contains the source files used in the finished DVD project. Notice that there are several different types of files in the project. In Adobe Encore DVD, you can work with many types of audio, video, and still image files.

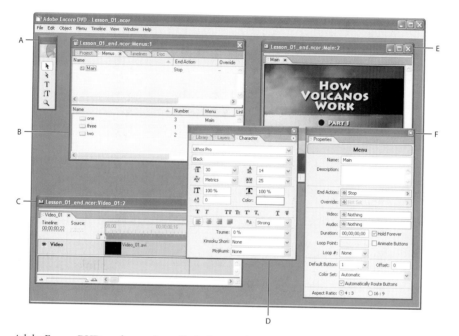

Adobe Encore DVD workspace (not all windows and palettes appear at all times)
A. *Toolbox* **B.** *Project window with Menus tab displayed* **C.** *Timeline window*
D. *Palette window* **E.** *Menu Editor window for selected menu* **F.** *Properties palette*

4 Choose File > Preview.

The Project Preview window opens, and a video plays for a few seconds. Then a DVD menu appears. You can use the Project Preview window to preview a viewer's experience of a DVD project—including navigation, links, and other behaviors—before you burn a disc.

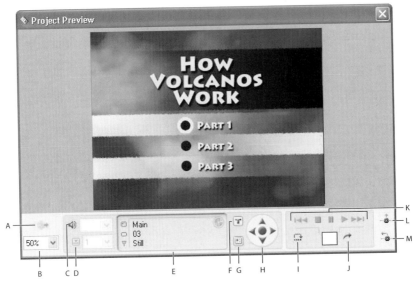

Project Preview window
A. Render Current Motion Menu B. Display Area Zoom C. Cycle Through Audio Tracks
D. Cycle Through Subtitle Tracks E. Status Area F. Remote Control Title Button G. Remote Control Menu Button H. Arrow
and Enter Keys I. Execute End Action J. Go to Entered Chapter K. Playback Controls
L. Exit Here M. Exit and Return

5 Move the cursor over the buttons next to the chapter names. As you move the cursor over a button, a white border appears around it.

6 Click the Part 1 button.

A video plays for approximately a minute. There are three distinct parts—or chapters—in the video; the menu links to each of them. When the video has finished playing, the menu reappears.

The Project Preview window has controls that represent those found on a television DVD player's remote control.

7 Click the up and down arrows until the Part 3 button is highlighted. Then click the Part 3 button.

The third part of the video plays. When it is finished, the menu reappears.

8 Close the Project Preview window and the Lesson_01_end Project window.

Planning your DVD

Now you'll create the same DVD project you just previewed. You will import video and audio files as assets, and a layered Photoshop file as a menu. Following the organization shown in the diagram below, you will create links from buttons to chapter points in the video timeline, and then set behaviors for those links.

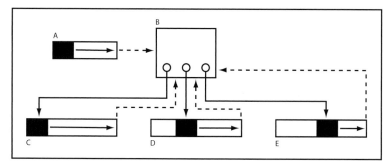

The Introduction timeline (A) plays when the DVD is inserted, and then the Main menu (B) opens. When the first button is activated, the Video_1 timeline (C) plays from beginning to end, and then the Main menu reappears. When the second button is activated, the Video_1 timeline plays from the Chapter 2 marker (D) to the end, and then the Main menu reappears. When the third button is activated, the Video_1 timeline plays from the Chapter 3 marker (E) to the end, and then the Main menu reappears.

You might find it helpful to organize your project with simple flow charts.

About flow charts

Regardless of the complexity of the project, it is helpful to work through the flow of your project and determine how the elements should link together before you begin creating it. Some DVD authors use flow charts, and some use spreadsheets. However you choose to plan your project, it is valuable to draft possible navigation scenarios and anticipate problems before you start. Sketching each of the elements and drawing the links between them can help you clarify how you want your project to be viewed.

Importing files as assets

You can use a variety of video, audio, and still image files in Adobe Encore DVD. You can import files into an Adobe Encore DVD project as either assets or menus. Assets are the files that make up the content of the DVD; menus display options to give viewers access to that content. First, you'll create a new Adobe Encore DVD project.

1 Choose File > New Project. Click OK to accept NTSC as the television standard.

A new Project window appears. Now you'll import assets into the Project window.

2 Choose File > Import as Asset.

3 In the Import as Asset dialog box, navigate to the Lesson 01 folder on your hard drive. Then hold down the Ctrl key while you select **Intro.m2v**, **Intro.wav**, and **Video_01.avi**. (Holding down the Ctrl key lets you select multiple files at once.)

4 Click Open.

The files you selected appear in the Project window.

5 Resize the Project window or move the scroll bar at the bottom of the window to view information about the files you imported. By default, the Project window displays the name, file type, size, path, and transcode settings for each file.

6 Choose File > Save As to save the project. Name it **Lesson_01.ncor**.

Creating a timeline

In Adobe Encore DVD, you assemble video, audio, and subtitle assets into timelines, where you can identify different sections of the video using chapter points. Each timeline contains a single video track. Start the project by creating a timeline for the Intro video.

1 Choose Timeline > New Timeline.

An untitled Timeline window appears, and the Monitor window opens. Notice that the untitled timeline is also listed in the Project window.

The Timeline window
A. *Current-time indicator* **B.** *I-Frames* **C.** *Chapter point* **D.** *Timeline tabs* **E.** *Timeline* **F.** *Source*
G. *Tracks* **H.** *Zoom slider*

You'll need to name the timeline. The Properties palette displays the attributes for the item currently selected. If the Properties palette isn't open, choose Window > Properties.

2 In the Name field of the Properties palette, type **Introduction**. (If you see attributes for something other than the timeline, click in the Timeline window to make the timeline active.)

3 Select the Intro.m2v file in the Project window, and drag it onto the video track in the Timeline window.

4 Select the Intro.wav file in the Project window, and drag it onto the Audio 1 track in the Timeline window.

You can view the current timeline in the Monitor window. Unlike the Project Preview window, the Monitor window displays only the video and audio tracks in the timeline; it does not display the DVD behavior. The Monitor window opens when you create a timeline.

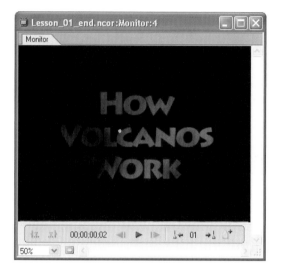

5 Click the Play button (►) in the Monitor window.

The introductory video plays for about eight seconds, and then ends.

6 Save the project.

Adding chapter points

Chapter points identify locations in the video track to which you want to link buttons or other navigational behaviors. You can add chapter points in the Timeline window.

In this project, you want to create links to three different chapter points in the Video_01 clip, so you need to add chapter points to the clip. First, you will create a new timeline for the Video_01.avi clip.

1 In the Project window, select the Video_01.avi file, and then click the Create a New Timeline button (▦) at the bottom of the Project window.

Adobe Encore DVD creates a new timeline named Video_01, and places the Video_01.avi file in the video and audio tracks.

A tab appears at the upper-left side of the Timeline window for each timeline in the project. Click a tab to view the corresponding timeline. For example, if you click the Introduction tab, the Introduction timeline appears.

2 Click the Video_01 tab to make sure the Video_01 timeline is active. Then click the Play button in the Monitor window to view the video. When it has finished, leave the Monitor window open.

3 Move the current-time indicator to the left edge of the timeline. The time displayed should be 00:00:00:00.

An initial chapter point is automatically created at the beginning of every timeline (that is, at 00:00:00:00).

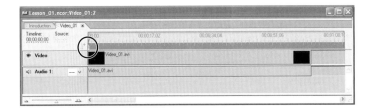

4 In the Timeline window, move the current-time indicator to the right until the time display shows 00:00:26:00.

To position the current-time indicator quickly, move the scroll bar at the bottom of the Timeline window until the destination time is visible. Then click on the time graph.

5 Choose Timeline > Add Chapter Point.

A chapter point marker with the number 2 appears on the timeline at 00:00:26:00, where the current-time indicator is positioned. The marker is automatically numbered.

6 In the Timeline window, move the current-time indicator to the right until the time displayed is 00:00:48:00. Then choose Timeline > Add Chapter Point again.

A marker with the number 3 appears on the timeline at 00:00:48:00.

You can also add a chapter point by pressing the asterisk key. This is a great way to add chapter points that correspond with audio cues.

7 Close the Timeline window and save the project. (The Monitor window closes automatically when you close the Timeline window.)

Importing a layered Photoshop file as a menu

One of the most powerful features of Adobe Encore DVD is its ability to import menus created in Photoshop. If you use Adobe Encore DVD naming conventions for layers in a Photoshop image, those layers remain intact when you import the file as a menu. You can make many changes and additions to the file directly in Adobe Encore DVD.

In this lesson, you'll import a Photoshop image that has already been created with layers using the Adobe Encore DVD naming conventions.

1 Choose File > Import as Menu.

2 In the Import as Menu dialog box, select **Main.psd**, and click Open.

The Menu Editor window opens, displaying the Main menu you imported. The Photoshop layers are intact. To see them in the Layers palette, choose Window > Layers.

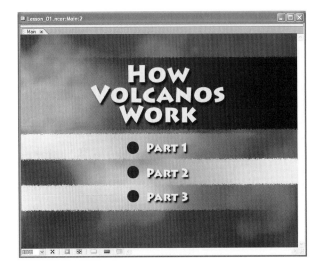

3 Select the selection tool ( ) in the toolbox. Then select Part 1 in the Menu Editor window.

A bounding box appears around the button and the text "Part 1."

4 If the Properties palette is not open, choose Window > Properties to open it. The Button Name field shows the name of the button: One.

5 Choose Video_01 > Chapter 1 from the Link pop-up menu.

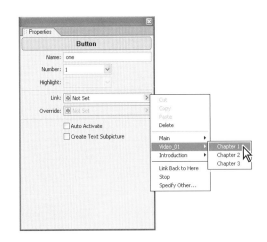

When the viewer clicks the Part 1 button on the DVD, Video_01 will play, beginning with the first chapter point, which was automatically created at the beginning of the timeline.

6 With the selection tool, select Part 2 in the Menu Editor window. In the Properties palette, choose Video_01 > Chapter 2 from the Link pop-up menu.

7 Using the same procedure, link the Part 3 button to Video_01 > Chapter 3.

8 Save the project.

Setting start and end behaviors

You have set links that viewers can use to start playing the video at specific chapter points. Now you need to define the sequences that aren't controlled by the viewer. For example, you need to determine which timeline or menu runs when the DVD is first inserted into the player, and which timeline or menu follows it.

For this project, you want the Introduction timeline to run when the viewer inserts the DVD. When it has finished playing, the main menu should appear.

1 In the Project window, select the Introduction timeline.

On the icon next to the Introduction timeline is a small circle with an arrow in it (📁). This symbol indicates that this item plays first when the DVD is inserted into the player.

Note: If the symbol doesn't appear on the icon next to the Introduction timeline, right-click the Introduction timeline in the Project window, and choose Set as First Play.

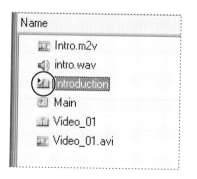

2 In the Properties palette, choose Main > One from the End Action pop-up menu.

When the Introduction timeline has finished playing, the Main menu will appear. The Part 1 button will be selected by default.

3 In the Project window, select the Video_01 timeline.

Note: Make sure you select the Video_01 timeline, and not Video_01.avi.

4 In the Properties palette, choose Main > One from the End Action pop-up menu.

When Video_01 has finished playing, the Main menu will appear. The Part 1 button will be selected by default.

5 Save the project.

Setting behaviors for remote control buttons

Next, you will define the behaviors for the Title and Menu buttons on a DVD player's remote control.

1 In the Project window, click an empty space to deselect all assets, timelines, or menus. The Disc attributes should appear in the Properties palette.

2 In the Properties palette, choose Introduction > Chapter 1 from the Title Button pop-up menu.

If the viewer clicks the Title button on the DVD player's remote control, the Introduction timeline will play. This setting is for the entire disc, no matter what is showing when the Title button is pressed.

3 Select the Introduction timeline in the Project window. In the Properties palette, choose Main > One from the Menu Remote pop-up menu.

If the viewer clicks the Menu button on the DVD player's remote control while the Introduction timeline is playing, the Main menu will appear, with the Part 1 button selected.

4 In the Project window, select the Video_01 timeline. In the Properties palette, choose Main > One from the Menu Remote pop-up menu.

If the viewer clicks the Menu button on the DVD player's remote control while the Video_01 timeline is playing, the Main menu will appear, with the Part 1 button selected.

5 Save the project.

Previewing the project

Before burning your DVD project to a disc, it's a good idea to make sure the project works as you expect it to. When you preview the DVD, you can test its sequencing and navigation, interacting with the DVD exactly as your audience will. The Project Preview window behaves just as if a disc has been inserted into a DVD player.

1 Choose File > Preview.

If the project is configured correctly, the Introduction timeline plays in the Project Preview window. When it has finished playing, the Main menu appears, and the Part 1 button is highlighted.

2 Click a button in the Main menu. The video should play from the appropriate chapter point, and then the Main menu should reappear, with the Part 1 button selected. Click each button to ensure that the video begins playing at the appropriate chapter point.

3 While the video is playing, click the Menu button (🔲) at the bottom of the Project Preview window. The Main menu should appear.

4 While the video is playing, click the Title button (🔳) at the bottom of the Project Preview window. The Introduction timeline should play.

5 Click the Exit and Return button (🔳) to close the Project Preview window and return to your project.

💡 *If you want to go directly from the Project Preview window to the timeline or menu currently displayed, click the Exit Here button (🔳).*

If the DVD project didn't behave as described above, return to the project and correct the behavior. Preview the DVD again to ensure that it behaves as expected before continuing.

Burning the DVD

You're ready to burn the DVD!

1 In the Project window, click the Disc tab.

The Disc tab lists the disc name, the space available on the disc, the type of media, and other information.

2 From the pop-up menu beneath the disc name, choose the data size of the disc you'll be burning.

3 Click Build Project.

4 In the Make DVD Disc dialog box, choose Current Project from the Create Using pop-up menu, and choose your DVD recorder from the Recorder pop-up menu.

If your recorder is not listed, verify that it is properly connected and installed. See the documentation for your recorder for assistance.

5 Insert a blank disc into the recorder, and click Next.

Note: If you click Next too quickly, you may see a Device Not Ready dialog box. Click OK to let your computer recognize the disc you inserted.

6 Review the information in the Make DVD Disc Summary dialog box. When you are ready to proceed, click Build.

Burning the disc may take several minutes, depending on the DVD recorder, the computer system, and the size of the media.

Review questions

1 What does the Project window show?

2 What is the difference between an imported asset and an imported menu?

3 Why would you create a chapter point?

4 How does the Monitor window differ from the Project Preview window?

Review answers

1 The Project window shows information about the assets, menus, timelines, and other objects included in the project.

2 An imported asset is used as content on the DVD. An imported menu is used as a menu from which viewers can navigate to content.

3 Create a chapter point to define a location in a video track to which you want to link a menu button or attach a behavior.

4 The Monitor window displays only the selected video track. The Project Preview window plays the entire DVD project, as if you were viewing it on a television DVD player.

Lesson 2

2 | Creating Menus in Adobe Encore DVD

Menus are the key to most DVD projects. Adobe Encore DVD provides all the tools you need to create menus without ever leaving the application. In this lesson, you'll type directly onto menus, import backgrounds, add buttons, and more.

In this lesson, you'll create a simple menu in Adobe Encore DVD, using imported assets as background and button files. You'll learn how to do the following:

- Create a new menu in Adobe Encore DVD.

- Import background files.

- Type text onto a menu.

- Format text, including font, size, character spacing, and color.

- Move objects on a menu.

- View the Title Safe area for a menu.

- Work with the Layers palette.

- Change the stacking order of layers.

- Add subpictures to your menu.

Getting started

In this lesson, you'll create a new Adobe Encore DVD project, using graphic and video files included on the *Adobe Encore DVD Classroom in a Book* DVD. Make sure you know the location of the files you need for Lesson 2. For help, see "Copying the Classroom in a Book files" on page 2.

Viewing the finished Adobe Encore DVD project

To see what you'll be creating, take a look at the finished project.

1 Start Adobe Encore DVD.

2 Choose File > Open Project.

3 In the Open dialog box, navigate to the Lesson 02 folder. Select **Lesson_02_end.ncor**, and then click Open.

4 Choose File > Preview.

The Project Preview window opens, and a DVD menu appears. There are three simple buttons.

5 Click the Valves button.

A short video plays. When the video has finished playing, the menu reappears.

6 Click each of the other buttons to play the other videos.

7 Close the Project Preview window and the Lesson_02_end Project window.

About menus

Menus make it possible to navigate through a DVD's contents: the video clips, still images, and audio clips. A single menu may serve as a table of contents for the entire disc, or the DVD may include multiple menus, serving different purposes at different points in the viewer's experience. For example, the main menu may link to menus that let you choose subtitle languages or different chapters in a video.

A menu consists of a background and buttons that link to assets. It may also contain subpictures, which change the appearance of a button when the viewer moves the mouse over it or selects it.

Menus can be as simple or as complex as you want them to be. You can create a menu entirely in Adobe Encore DVD, as you will in this lesson, or you can design a menu in Adobe Photoshop and import it into your DVD project. (You'll use Photoshop to create a menu in Lesson 3.)

Creating a new menu

You'll create a menu in Adobe Encore DVD. First, you will open a new project, and then you will add the menu.

1 Choose File > New Project. Click OK to accept NTSC as the television standard.

A new Project window appears. Now you'll create a new menu.

2 Choose Menu > New Menu.

The Menu Editor window appears, displaying the default menu, which is named NTSC_4 x 3 Blank Menu. Notice that the menu is also listed in the Project window.

The Menu Editor window is the work area for creating and editing menus in Adobe Encore DVD. You can place, move, resize, or delete buttons and subpictures in the Menu Editor window, and you can also add and format text. Use the buttons at the bottom of the Menu Editor window to change how the menu is displayed.

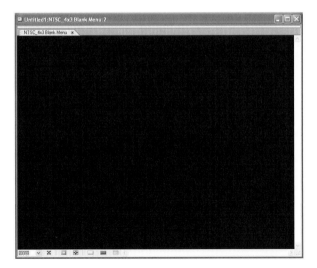

💡 *You can specify the default menu using the Library palette. You'll have the opportunity to specify the default menu in lesson 4. For this project, we'll use the menu that is the default when you first start Adobe Encore DVD.*

You'll need to name the menu, using the Properties palette. If the Properties palette isn't open, choose Window > Properties, or if it's hidden behind another palette, click the Properties tab to make it active.

3 Click in the Menu Editor window to ensure that it's active. Then type **Maintenance** in the Name field of the Properties palette.

4 Click in the Project window. The menu name is automatically updated in both the Project window and the tab in the Menu Editor window.

Note: There should be a circle with an arrow in it (🔊) on the icon next to the Maintenance menu in the Project window. This symbol indicates that the Maintenance menu will play first when the disc is inserted into the player. If the symbol isn't there, right-click the Maintenance menu, and choose Set as First Play.

5 Choose File > Save As to save the project. Name the project **Lesson_02.ncor**.

Adding text to a menu

Adobe Encore DVD provides advanced typographic control. Using the Character palette, you can kern, track, and scale text. You can also shift its baseline. You can set text attributes before you type characters, or you can style and format existing text. Adobe Encore DVD provides two text tools: one creates horizontal text and one creates vertical text. In this project, you'll type horizontal text directly into the menu, and then move it to the appropriate position.

1 Select the text tool (T) from the toolbox, and click in the Menu Editor window.

A blinking insertion point appears.

2 Type **Horn Maintenance**.

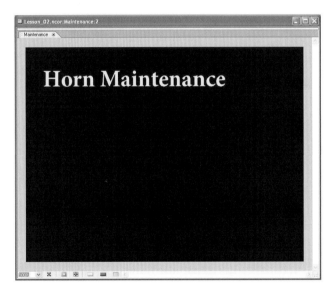

3 Choose Edit > Select All to select the text you just typed.

Note: If the text isn't selected, click in the text and then choose Edit > Select All again.

4 Make the Character palette active by clicking the Character tab or, if the palette isn't open, by choosing Window > Character.

5 Choose Minion Pro for the font, Bold for the font style, and 60 for the type size. Click the Align Left option.

As you specify options in the Character palette, the selected text changes.

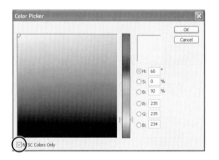

6 Click the Color box and select white (in the upper-left corner). Select NTSC Colors Only. Click OK to close the Color Picker.

The NTSC color set is a subset of colors optimized for television viewing.

You've created a text block using the text tool to type and format text. Now you want to position the text block. To manipulate the text block as an object, you'll use the selection tool.

7 Select the selection tool ( ) in the toolbox.

8 Drag the text block to the top center of the menu.

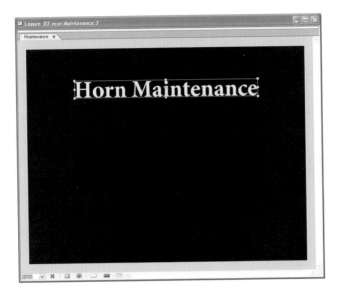

9 Click in the Menu Editor window to deselect the text block.

Changes you make in the Character palette affect only the selected text. If no text is selected when you make the changes, the settings become the default settings for new text. Now you'll set the defaults for the button text.

10 In the Character palette, choose Minion Pro for the font, Bold Condensed for the font style, and 36 for the type size.

11 Select the text tool and click in the Menu Editor window.

12 Type **Valves**, and select the selection tool to deselect the text.

The Character attributes you set as defaults were automatically applied to the text.

13 Select the text tool again, and click an insertion point in the menu. Type **Slides,** and select the selection tool again.

14 Select the text tool again, click an insertion point, and type **Cleaning**.

You should have three separate text blocks.

15 Choose View > Show Safe Area, or click the Show Safe Area button () at the bottom of the Menu Editor window.

A border appears inside the menu, representing the Title Safe area—the part of the menu that will be visible on a television screen. Keep all the text inside that border to ensure that all viewers can access buttons and read the text.

16 With the selection tool, drag the text blocks you just created toward the lower-left corner of the menu, within the Title Safe area.

17 Save the project.

Adding assets to menus

Menu backgrounds can contain a single layer (such as the menu you used in the first lesson) or multiple layers. When you want to include objects in your menu, import them as assets.

1 Right-click in the Project window, and select Import as Asset.

2 Navigate to the Lesson 02 folder. Then hold down the Ctrl key while you select **Gradients.psd**, **Valves.avi**, **Slides.avi**, and **Cleaning.avi**.

You can use the Shift key to select contiguous files. Click Cleaning.avi, then press the Shift key and click Valves.avi. The files between them are also selected.

3 Click Open.

The files you selected appear in the Project window.

4 Enlarge the Menu Editor window until you can see the edges of the menu. (A gray background appears behind the black menu.)

5 Drag the Gradients.psd file from the Project window into the Menu Editor window. With the selection tool, position the new layer to fill the menu.

The Gradients.psd file is a Photoshop file with a single layer. As you move the Gradients.psd file over the menu, it retains its transparency, so you can see the default menu and the text you created behind it. Adobe Encore DVD honors transparency in Photoshop files because Adobe Encore DVD and Photoshop use the same graphics engine.

6 Open the Layers palette by choosing Windows > Layers or clicking the Layers tab in the palette set.

The Layers palette contains several layers. Each text block you created is on its own layer, as is the Gradients.psd file. The Layers palette in Adobe Encore DVD is similar to the Layers palette in Photoshop. You can use it to organize and edit your menu in Adobe Encore DVD at any time until you burn the DVD.

7 Select the Gradients.psd layer in the Layers palette. Then choose Object > Arrange > Send to Back.

The Gradients layer moves beneath the text layers, and its order changes in the Layers palette. Use the Arrange commands to change the stacking order of objects in your menu.

8 Open Windows Explorer: right-click the Start menu and choose Explore.

9 Arrange your screen so that you can see both Adobe Encore DVD and Windows Explorer.

10 Drag the **Background.psd** file from the Lesson 02 folder in Windows Explorer into the Menu Editor window in Adobe Encore DVD. Use the selection tool to position the new layer so that it fills the menu.

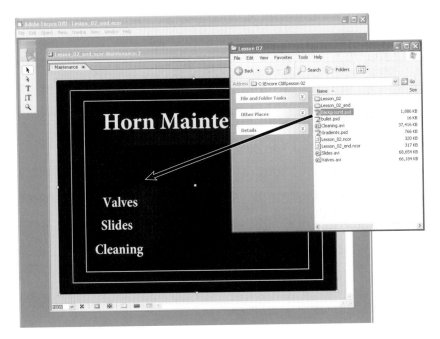

11 With the Background.psd layer selected, choose Object > Arrange > Send to Back.

💡 *To keep layers from moving after you position them, click the middle box next to the layer name in the Layers palette, so that a padlock icon appears. When a layer is locked, you cannot modify it.*

Adding drop shadows to text

You'll add drop shadows to the title and each of the text buttons. First, you'll position them within the maroon stripes.

1 With the selection tool, position the title in the first maroon stripe.

2 With the selection tool, select the three text blocks that you will use as buttons. Press Ctrl to select multiple text blocks.

3 Position the text blocks within the wide maroon stripe.

4 Select one text layer in the Layers palette, and then press the Ctrl key while you select the others.

Note: There are four text layers. Be sure to select them all.

5 Choose Object > Drop Shadow. Click OK to accept the default settings.

Drop shadows appear for all the text in the menu.

6 Save the project.

Converting text blocks to buttons

Now you're ready to create buttons for the menu. In Adobe Encore DVD, you can create buttons from moving or still images you import, or text you type into a menu—or you can use predesigned buttons from the Library palette. For this project, you'll convert the text blocks you created earlier into buttons.

1 With the direct select tool, select the three text blocks. (Press the Ctrl key to select multiple objects.)

2 Choose Object > Align > Left.

The text blocks are aligned on the left side, matching the left edge of the first text block you selected.

3 Then choose Object > Distribute > Vertically.

The text blocks are distributed so that the vertical spaces between them are equal.

4 With the text blocks still selected, choose Object > Convert to Button.

The appearance of the text blocks in the Menu Editor window doesn't change, but the names of the layers in the Layers palette do. Adobe Encore DVD uses special naming conventions for buttons, which can be linked to timelines or other menus.

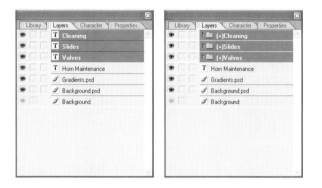

5 Save the project.

Adding subpictures to buttons

A subpicture is a graphic overlay that you can use to change the appearance of a button when the viewer moves the mouse over it or selects it. You can create subpictures from buttons in Adobe Encore DVD.

1 With the selection tool, select a button in the Menu Editor window.

2 Choose Object > Create Subpicture.

Adobe Encore DVD creates a new layer, with the same shape as the button. Its name begins with (=), which indicates that it is a subpicture layer.

3 Choose View > Show Selected Subpicture to see how the button will look when it's activated. Or click the Show Selected Subpicture button () on the Menu Editor window.

4 Repeat steps 1 and 2 to create subpictures for the other two buttons.

Assigning color groups for subpictures

When you add subpictures to buttons, the default subpicture colors are applied. To apply different colors to the subpictures, first create a new color set, and then assign that color set to the menu. You'll create a new color set for this menu.

1 Choose Edit > Color Sets > Menu.

2 In the Menu Color Set dialog box, click the New Color Set button.

3 In the New Color Set dialog box, type **Horn Color Set,** and click OK to return to the Menu Color Set dialog box.

4 In the Highlight Group 1 section, click the Color 1 swatch.

The Color Picker opens.

5 Choose a red color, or type **215**, **35**, and **56** in the R, G, and B fields, respectively. Select NTSC Colors Only. Click OK.

6 In the Highlight Group 1 section, choose 80% from the Opacity pop-up menu next to the Color 1 swatch. Click OK.

7 In the Project window, select the Maintenance menu to make it active.

8 In the Properties palette, choose Horn Color Set from the Color Set pop-up menu.

The new subpicture color appears in the Menu Editor window.

Note: If you don't see the subpicture color, click the Show Selected Subpicture button on the Menu Editor window.

Linking buttons to timelines

Now you'll link the buttons you've created to the video clips. First, you'll create timelines for the video files you imported earlier.

1 Press the Ctrl key while you select the three AVI files in the Project window.

2 Click the New Timeline button () at the bottom of the Project window.

The Timeline window opens, with tabs for three timelines. Each AVI file is automatically placed in its own timeline. The timelines are added to the Project window. The Monitor window also opens.

3 In the Project window, select the three timelines. Then open the Properties palette by clicking the Properties tab or choosing Window > Properties.

Note: Make sure you select the timelines, and not the AVI files, in the Project window.

4 In the Properties palette, choose Maintenance > Default from the End Action pop-up menu.

The end action determines what happens after the timeline finishes playing. Here, the DVD will return to the Maintenance menu after each video is finished.

$\bigcirc$ *If you want every timeline to return to the main menu after it finishes playing, you can save time by selecting all the timelines and then setting the end action once. The end action will be applied to all the timelines you've selected.*

5 Use the selection tool to select the Valves button in the Menu Editor window.

6 In the Properties palette, choose Valves > Chapter 1 from the Link pop-up menu.

The button you selected is now linked to the Valves timeline. When the viewer clicks the Valves button, the Valves timeline will play.

Note: The link is assigned to Chapter 1, even though you didn't create any chapter points in the Valves timeline. Every timeline has a chapter point—named Chapter 1—at its beginning.

7 Repeat steps 5–6 for the other two buttons, linking each button to its corresponding timeline.

8 Save the project.

Previewing the project

Before you burn a DVD, make sure the project is configured properly. It should look and behave just like the one you previewed at the beginning of this lesson.

1 Choose File > Preview.

If the project is configured correctly, the Maintenance menu appears. The Valves button is selected by default, so its subpicture appears.

2 Click one of the buttons. The appropriate video should play, and when it's finished, you should return to the Maintenance menu.

3 Click the other two buttons. Each video should play, and then return you to the Maintenance menu.

4 Close the Project Preview window.

If the DVD project didn't behave as described above, return to the project and correct the behavior. Preview the DVD again to ensure that it behaves as expected before continuing.

Adobe Encore DVD folder structure

As you create a project, Adobe Encore DVD stores the menus and assets you use in a project folder. Within the project folder are two subfolders, named Cache and Sources. Adobe Encore DVD uses the Cache folder as you work in the project; it stores your original menus and assets in the Sources folder. Additionally, the preferences for your project are stored in a ProjectPrefs.xml file in the project folder.

If you need to move a DVD project to a different computer, make sure you move the entire project folder and all its contents. Otherwise, Adobe Encore DVD will not be able to find the files it needs to open the project.

Burning the DVD

You're ready to burn the DVD.

1 In the Project window, select the Disc tab.

The Disc tab lists the disc name, the space available on the disc, the media type, and other information.

2 Choose the data size of the disc you'll be burning from the pop-up menu beneath the disc name.

Notice that both the amount of disc space used by the project and the resulting available disc space are listed beneath the data size of the disc. Additionally, Adobe Encore DVD shows the amount of space used for content, as opposed to disk formatting.

3 Click Check Links, and then select the link problems you want to search for. Click OK to begin the search. Click Done after you've examined the results.

If there are link problems that will cause the DVD to play incorrectly, return to the project and fix them before burning the disc.

Adobe Encore DVD can identify broken links, unset links, and timelines or menus to which there is no navigational link. For more information about checking links, see "Finding missing links and unassigned assets" in Adobe Encore DVD Help.

4 Click Build Project. Click Save and Continue if you are prompted to save the file.

5 In the Make DVD Disc dialog box, choose Current Project from the Create Using pop-up menu, and choose your DVD recorder from the Recorder pop-up menu.

If your recorder is not listed, verify that it is properly connected and installed. See the documentation for your recorder for assistance.

6 Insert a blank disc into the recorder, and click Next.

7 Review the information in the Make DVD Disc Summary dialog box. When you are ready to proceed, click Build.

Burning the disc may take several minutes, depending on the DVD recorder, the computer system, and the size of the media.

Understanding bit budgeting

Bit budgeting, or estimating the amount of space your project will occupy on DVD, is an important part of planning. Bit budgeting helps you strike a balance between the quantity and quality of content and determine the optimal video data rate. If your DVD includes minimal amounts of content, you can encode that content at a higher data rate (which translates to higher quality) to take advantage of all available space on the DVD.

Conversely, if your project contains a large amount of content, you need to use a lower data rate (which translates to lower quality) to squeeze it all onto the DVD.

Adobe Encore DVD automatically tracks bit budgeting during the authoring process. For small projects with limited content, simply checking the amount of available space on the Disc tab during the authoring process is usually sufficient to track your space usage. For large, complex projects, though, bit budgeting becomes much more important to the authoring process. For more information about bit budgeting, see "Understanding bit budgeting" in Adobe Encore DVD Help.

Review questions

1 Which tool do you use to create text?

2 Which tool do you use to move a text block?

3 What is the Title Safe area in a menu?

4 How do you change the stacking order of layers?

5 How do you add a drop shadow to text?

6 When might you use a subpicture?

7 What are two ways to display the Layers palette?

Review answers

1 Use the text tool or the vertical text tool to type or format text.

2 Use the selection tool to move a text block, resize it, or otherwise manipulate it as an object.

3 The Title Safe area is the area that will appear on every viewer's television or computer monitor, so you can be sure that content in that area will be visible.

4 Select a layer in the Layers palette, choose Object > Arrange, and then choose Bring to Front, Send to Back, Bring Forward, or Send Backward.

5 Select the text layer in the Layers palette, and then choose Object > Drop Shadow.

6 You can use a subpicture to change a button's appearance when the viewer mouses over or selects it.

7 Choose Window > Layers or, if the Layers palette is open but not active, click the Layers tab in the palette set.

Lesson 3

3 | Designing Menus in Adobe Photoshop

Adobe Encore DVD is designed to work seamlessly with Adobe Photoshop. You can take advantage of the numerous layer styles and other design features in Photoshop to create exactly the menu you want, and know that it will retain its appearance and formatting when you import it into Adobe Encore DVD.

In this lesson, you'll create a simple menu for Adobe Encore DVD using the powerful features of Adobe Photoshop. You'll see how the two applications work together seamlessly as you learn to do the following:

• Create a new menu in Photoshop.

• Compose a background for the menu from multiple images.

• Create text in Photoshop.

• Format and position text in Photoshop.

• Apply layer styles to text and image layers.

• Create and name buttons.

• Create and name subpictures.

• Edit the original Photoshop file from within Adobe Encore DVD.

• Burn a DVD using the Make DVD Disc command.

Getting started

In this lesson, you'll assemble images and type in a layered Photoshop file, create buttons using layer sets, and import the file as a menu in Adobe Encore DVD. Then you'll use tools in Adobe Encore DVD to modify the menu and link its buttons to timelines.

All the graphic and video files required for this lesson are included on the *Adobe Encore DVD Classroom in a Book* DVD. Make sure you know the location of the files you need for Lesson 3. For help, see "Copying the Classroom in a Book files" on page 2.

You'll also need to have Adobe Photoshop 7.0 or later installed to complete this lesson.

Viewing the finished Adobe Encore DVD project

To see what you'll be creating, take a look at the finished project.

1 Start Adobe Encore DVD.

2 Choose File > Open Project.

3 In the Open dialog box, navigate to the Lesson 03 folder. Select **Lesson_03_end.ncor**, and then click Open.

4 Choose File > Preview.

The Project Preview window opens, and a DVD menu appears. There are three buttons in the shape of animals, and the giraffe is highlighted.

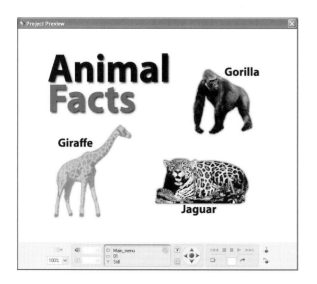

5 Click the Giraffe button.

A short video plays. When the video has finished playing, the menu reappears.

6 Click the Gorilla button, and then the Jaguar button, to play the other videos.

7 Close the Project Preview window and the Lesson_03_end Project window.

Teaming Adobe Encore DVD with Photoshop

As you've seen in the first two lessons, Adobe Encore DVD shares some features with Photoshop. For example, it includes a limited Layers palette, and you can create and edit text for menus. However, you can create more sophisticated, fully integrated menus using the robust graphic design features in Photoshop. Other DVD authoring applications flatten Photoshop files, making final edits cumbersome. Because Adobe Encore DVD preserves the layer information in the Photoshop file, you can return to Photoshop to edit your menu until the moment you burn the DVD.

Most DVD designers create menus in Photoshop, taking advantage of its extensive tool set. You can apply layer styles in Photoshop that are not available in Adobe Encore DVD, create adjustment layers, and format text using advanced formatting features. When you import the menu into Adobe Encore DVD, it recognizes and retains layer styles, and honors adjustment layers. Additionally, text you've formatted in Photoshop appears exactly the same in Adobe Encore DVD.

For a smooth workflow, you can return to Photoshop quickly using the Edit in Photoshop command from Adobe Encore DVD.

Note: You can use either Photoshop CS or Photoshop 7.0 to complete this lesson. Because Photoshop CS provides additional features for working with images intended for video, some steps are slightly different. Where necessary, separate instructions are provided for the two versions of Photoshop.

Creating a menu background in Photoshop

To create a menu in Photoshop, you'll create a new image and apply a background color to it.

1 In Photoshop, choose File > New.

2 From the Preset Sizes pop-up menu in the New dialog box, choose 720 x 534 Std. NTSC DV/DVD (Photoshop 7.0) or NTSC DV 720 x 480 (with guides) (Photoshop CS). In Photoshop CS, make sure the Pixel Aspect Ratio is set to D1/DV NTSC (0.9).

NTSC video has pixel dimensions of 720 x 480, but the Photoshop 7.0 file has more vertical pixels (534). This is because NTSC video is composed of non-square pixels. Photoshop 7.0 works only with square pixels, but you can import a 720 x 534 square-pixel image into Adobe Encore DVD, and it is automatically scaled to fit the proper pixel aspect ratio.

Photoshop CS lets you create an image with non-square pixels, so Adobe Encore DVD doesn't need to scale the image when you import it.

You don't have to memorize the pixel dimensions; just remember which preset to choose when you create a new menu.

Choose the preset in the New dialog box in Photoshop 7.0 (left) or Photoshop CS (right).

Square pixels and rectangular pixels

If you create menus or backgrounds using square pixels, it is best to size them using the Photoshop preset image sizes. When Adobe Encore DVD builds the DVD, it automatically compensates for the change in pixel dimensions. Thus, when the viewer plays the DVD in the rectangular pixel environment of the television, the menus will not appear squashed.

3 Name the image Main, choose RGB Color from the Mode pop-up menu, and then click OK to close the New dialog box.

If you are using Photoshop CS, the image opens with guides for the Action Safe and Title Safe areas. To turn the guides off, choose View > Clear Guides.

4 Choose File > Save As, choose Photoshop (*.PSD, *.PDD) from the Format pop-up menu, specify the folder into which to save the file, and click OK.

The file is named Main.psd and is saved to the folder you specified. Note where you saved the file, so you can find it when you need to import it into Adobe Encore DVD later.

5 Choose File > Open. Navigate to the Lesson 03 folder in the Open dialog box. Then hold down the Ctrl key while you select **Small_giraffe.psd**, **Small_gorilla.psd**, and **Small_jaguar.psd**. Click Open.

Note: You may see a dialog box about color management. For this project, you don't need to use color management. However, you may want to use color management in your DVD projects to achieve the best results. To learn more about color management, refer to your Photoshop user guide.

The three animal files you selected open in Photoshop. The Main.psd file is still open as well.

6 Arrange the windows so that both the Main.psd and Small_giraffe.psd files are visible.

7 Click the Small_giraffe.psd file to make it the active file. With the move tool ( ), drag the image of the giraffe into the Main.psd file.

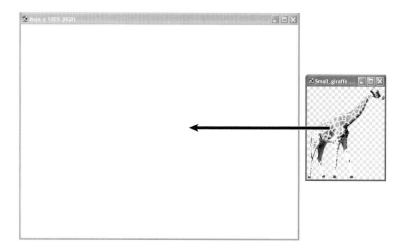

A new layer appears in the Layers palette; it's named Giraffe image.

8 Use the move tool to position the Giraffe layer in the lower-left area of the image.

9 Arrange the windows so that both the Main.psd and Small_gorilla.psd files are visible.

10 Click the Small_gorilla.psd file to make it the active file. With the move tool, drag the image of the gorilla into the Main.psd file. Then move the Gorilla layer to the right side of the image.

The Gorilla image layer appears in the Layers palette.

11 Click the Small_Jaguar.psd file, and use the move tool to drag it into the Main.psd file. Position it at the bottom of the image area.

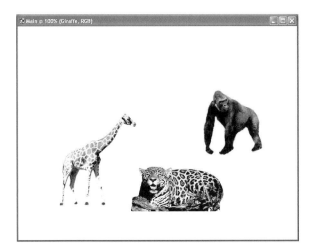

12 Click the Main.psd file to ensure that it's the active file. Choose File > Save to save it. Then close the Small_giraffe.psd, Small_gorilla.psd, and Small_jaguar.psd files without saving them.

Note: In Photoshop CS, the Photoshop Format options dialog box may appear; click OK.

Creating text in Photoshop

Photoshop provides more text formatting tools than Adobe Encore DVD, so you can get just the effect you want. Adobe Encore DVD recognizes the formatting and displays the text correctly—and you can always return to Photoshop to edit the text or its formatting.

You can type text directly into a Photoshop image, and then quickly change its formatting or its position. Use options in the Character palette and the Paragraph palette to format the text. Use the move tool when you want to move a text block.

1 Select the horizontal type tool (T) from the toolbox, and then choose Window > Character to open the Character palette. By default, the Paragraph palette is docked with the Character palette.

2 Choose Myriad Pro for the font, Bold for the font style, and 30 for the type size.

3 Make sure that the foreground color is black. The foreground and background colors are shown in the toolbox. If the foreground color (the first box shown) is white, click the double-arrow icon to switch the two colors.

💡 *If the colors in the toolbox are not black and white, press the D key on your keyboard to quickly set the colors to the default foreground (black) and background (white) colors.*

4 Click the Giraffe image layer in the Layers palette to select it. Then click an insertion point to the left of the giraffe in the Main.psd window.

5 Type the word **Giraffe**, and press Ctrl+Enter.

A new text layer appears in the Layers palette. Pressing Ctrl+Enter releases the horizontal type tool from the text block so that you can create a new one.

6 Select the move tool, and then drag the text block to the position shown here.

7 Select the Gorilla image layer in the Layers palette. Then, with the horizontal type tool, click an insertion point to the right of the gorilla's head.

8 Type the word **Gorilla**, and press Ctrl+Enter.

9 Select the Jaguar image layer in the Layers palette. Then type the word **Jaguar** just below the image of the jaguar, and press Ctrl+Enter.

10 Select the move tool.

11 Select the Jaguar text layer in the Layers palette, and move it to the position shown below.

12 Select the Gorilla text layer in the Layers palette, and move it to the position shown below.

Note: The Classroom in a Book lesson files are designed to work with either Photoshop 7.0 or Photoshop CS. The sizes and proportions of the image elements on your monitor may appear slightly different from those in this book, depending on the version of Photoshop you are using and whether Pixel Aspect Ratio Correction is on or off. For this lesson, those differences are not critical.

13 Choose File > Save.

Changing the color of text in Photoshop

The animal names are black. Now you'll create the title for the menu, and you'll apply different colors.

1 With the horizontal type tool, click an insertion point in the upper-left area of the image.

2 In the Character palette, change the type size and leading; leave the other settings as they are. If you are using Photoshop 7.0, type **100 pt** for the type size and **90 pt** for the leading. If you are using Photoshop CS, type **80 pt** for the type size and **64 pt** for the leading.

3 Click the Paragraph tab to make the Paragraph palette active, and then click the Left Align Text option.

4 Type **Animal** and press Enter. Then type the word **Facts**, as shown here.

Note: In Photoshop CS, the text may not appear smooth if Pixel Aspect Ratio Correction is enabled. The text will appear as expected in Adobe Encore DVD.

5 With the horizontal type tool, double-click the word "Facts" to select it.

6 Click the Foreground color in the toolbox.

The Color Picker opens.

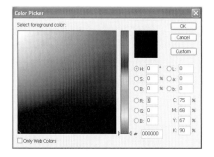

7 Click in the upper-right corner of the color field to select a bright red color. If you prefer, you can specify the color numerically in the Color Picker. (We used R=205, G=0, B=0.) Click OK.

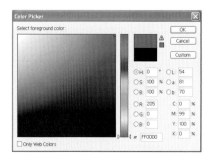

8 Press Ctrl+Enter to deselect the text.

The word "Facts" is now red.

9 Choose File > Save.

Applying layer styles in Photoshop

You can enhance a layer by adding a shadow, glow, bevel, emboss, or other special effect from a collection of automated and editable layer styles. In Adobe Encore DVD, you can apply a drop shadow effect, but there are many more layer styles available in Photoshop. Adobe Encore DVD recognizes the layer styles you apply in Photoshop, so it displays the effects accurately, and you can return to Photoshop to edit the layer styles at any time.

You'll apply a drop shadow effect to the Animal Facts text block.

1 Select the Animal Facts text layer in the Layers palette. Choose Layer > Layer Style > Drop Shadow.

The Layer Style dialog box appears. It includes more options for the drop shadow effect than the similar dialog box in Adobe Encore DVD, but the effect you apply in Photoshop will appear the same in Adobe Encore DVD.

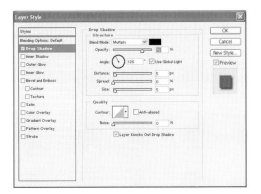

2 Leave the settings at their default values, and click OK.

The text appears with a drop shadow.

Now you will apply a different layer style to create a glowing outline for the animal images.

3 Select the Giraffe image layer in the Layers palette.

Note: Be sure to select the Giraffe image layer and not the Giraffe text layer.

4 Click the Add a Layer Style button at the bottom of the Layers palette, and choose Outer Glow.

The Layer Style dialog box appears, displaying the options for the Outer Glow layer style.

5 In the Layer Style dialog box, choose Normal from the Blend Mode pop-up menu.

6 Position the Layer Style dialog box so that you can see the word "Facts" in your image. Click the small color swatch in the Structure section of the Layer Style dialog box to open the Color Picker.

7 If necessary, move the Color Picker so that you can see the word "Facts" in your image. With the Color Picker open, move the cursor over the word "Facts" until it turns into the eyedropper tool ( ). Click on the word "Facts." Click OK to close the Color Picker.

To learn more about using the Color Picker, see "Using the Adobe Color Picker" in Photoshop Help.

The eyedropper tool selected the color you applied to the word "Facts," so you can use that color in the Layer Style dialog box, too.

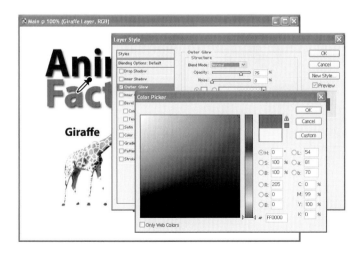

8 Click OK to close the Layer Style dialog box.

A red glow appears around the giraffe.

9 Repeat steps 3–8 for the Gorilla image layer and the Jaguar image layer, so that a red glow appears around all three animals.

10 Choose File > Save.

About layer styles

You can apply shadows, glows, bevels, embossed effects, and more using layer styles in Photoshop. These effects are linked to the contents of the layer—and when you move or edit the contents, the effects change as well. For example, if you apply a drop shadow to a text layer, the shadow changes automatically when you edit the text.

When a style is applied to a layer, an icon ( ) appears just to the right of the layer's name in the Layers palette in Photoshop. You can expand the style in the Layers palette to view all the effects that make up the style, and edit the effects to change the style.

Photoshop includes numerous predefined styles. You can create a custom style by applying multiple effects to a layer.

Creating buttons in Photoshop

Now you're ready to create buttons for the menu. In Lesson 2, you converted layers into buttons in Adobe Encore DVD. When you create a button from a layer, Adobe Encore DVD converts that layer into a layer set, using a specific naming convention. Likewise, Adobe Encore DVD recognizes buttons you create in Photoshop, as long as you name and organize their layers and layer sets properly.

1 Select the Giraffe text layer in the Layers palette, and choose Layer > New > Layer Set.

2 Name the layer set (+) **Giraffe Button**, and then click OK.

The layer set appears in the Layers palette, above the Giraffe text layer. It is important that the name begins with (+). Adobe Encore DVD recognizes layer sets whose names begin with (+) as buttons.

Now you'll move the Giraffe image layer and the Giraffe text layer into the new layer set.

3 In the Layers palette, drag the Giraffe text layer onto the folder for the (+) Giraffe Button layer set.

When you release the mouse button, the Giraffe text layer appears slightly indented below the Giraffe Button layer set in the Layers palette, meaning that it is included in the layer set.

4 Drag the Giraffe image layer onto the folder for the (+) Giraffe Button layer set.

Because the name of the layer set begins with (+), Adobe Encore DVD will recognize any layer in that set as part of the button.

5 Repeat steps 1– 4 to create a (+) Gorilla Button layer set that contains the Gorilla image layer and the Gorilla text layer.

6 Repeat steps 1– 4 to create a (+) Jaguar Button layer set that contains the Jaguar image layer and the Jaguar text layer.

7 Choose File > Save.

Menu Item	Photoshop Element	Layer Name Prefix	Example
Button name	Layer set containing button components	(+)	(+) Daisy button 1
Button text	Text layers within the layer set	None required	Daisy button
Button image	Image layers within the layer set	None required	Daisy image
Subpicture	Single-color image layers. Each layer represents one color of the three-color sub-picture.	(=1) (=2) (=3)	(=1)Text highlight (=2) Daisy outline (=3) Check mark
Video thumbnail	An image layer within the layer set that serves as a placeholder for video.	(%)	(%) Daisy thumbnail
Other design elements or text (such as logo or menu title)	Individual layer	None required	Summer flowers

Use the Adobe Encore DVD naming conventions when you create Photoshop layers and layer sets to ensure that Adobe Encore DVD recognizes buttons, subpictures, and thumbnails in the imported menu.

Add subpictures to buttons

In Lesson 2, you converted a layer into a subpicture, and Adobe Encore DVD changed the layer's name to follow a specific naming convention. You can create subpictures in Photoshop by following that same naming convention when you name layers. When you then import the file as a menu, Adobe Encore DVD automatically recognizes the subpictures.

A subpicture changes the appearance of a button when the viewer mouses over or activates it.

1 Select the Giraffe image layer in the Layers palette, and then choose Layer > Duplicate Layer.

2 In the Duplicate Layer dialog box, type (=1) for the layer name, and click OK.

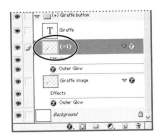

Photoshop adds a copy of the Giraffe image layer named (=1) to the (+) Giraffe Button layer set. If the new layer is not inside the (+) Giraffe Button layer set, drag it onto the layer set in the Layers palette. It is important that the layer's name begins (=1). Adobe Encore DVD recognizes layers whose names begin with (=) as subpictures.

The new subpicture layer is a copy of the Giraffe image layer, so it includes the Outer Glow layer style. You will remove the layer style from the new layer.

3 In the Layers palette, select the (=1) layer you just created, and choose Layer > Layer Style > Clear Layer Style.

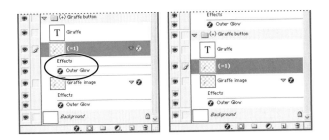

4 With the (=1) layer still selected in the Layers palette, click the Lock Transparent Pixels button at the top of the Layers palette.

When this button is selected, only the pixels of the giraffe image—not the transparent background—can change.

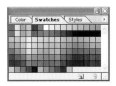

5 Choose Window > Swatches to open the Swatches palette. Select a light orange or yellow swatch.

The swatch you select becomes the foreground color.

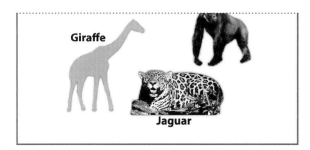

6 Choose Edit > Fill. In the Fill dialog box, choose Foreground Color from the Use pop-up menu, and set the Opacity value to 100%. Then click OK.

7 The giraffe image is filled with the foreground color.

If the entire layer is filled with the foreground color, choose Edit > Undo, click the Lock Transparent Pixels button in the Layers palette, and choose Edit > Fill again.

8 With the (=1) layer selected in the Layers palette, type **60** in the Opacity field.

The Giraffe image layer shows through the subpicture layer. Adobe Encore DVD will use the color and transparency values of the Photoshop layer when it creates subpictures.

9 Repeat steps 1–8 to create subpictures for the Gorilla image layer and the Jaguar image layer.

10 Save the file.

Importing a menu into Adobe Encore DVD

When you create a menu in Photoshop using the proper naming conventions, all you need to do is to import the menu into Adobe Encore DVD. Adobe Encore DVD automatically recognizes buttons, subpictures, and the effects you've applied in Photoshop.

You've created a Photoshop file to use as a menu in Adobe Encore DVD. To ensure that the buttons and their subpictures appear correctly, verify that the following is true:

• There are three layer sets, with names that begin (+).

• In each layer set, there is an image layer, a text layer, and a subpicture layer.

• Each subpicture layer has a name that begins (=1).

• The subpicture layers each have an opacity of 60%.

• No layer style is applied to the subpicture layers.

• The Animal Facts layer is not included in any layer set.

If you are unsure whether your file meets these criteria, compare it with the Photoshop file named Lesson_03_end.psd in the Lesson 03 folder. If the layers are named and organized appropriately, you're ready to import the menu into Adobe Encore DVD.

1 In Adobe Encore DVD, choose File > New Project. Click OK to accept NTSC as the television standard.

2 Choose File > Import as Menu. Select the **Main.psd** file you just created, and click OK.

The Menu Editor window opens. The Main file appears exactly as you created it in Photoshop. You can still edit the text in Adobe Encore DVD or in Photoshop. Adobe Encore DVD retains the layer styles, including the drop shadow on the title text and the outer glow applied to the animal images. The subpictures you created may not be visible; to see them, click one of the Show Subpicture buttons. Adobe Encore DVD interprets those layers with (=1) in their names as subpictures only.

Note: If you created the menu file in Photoshop CS, it may appear to be stretched horizontally. Click the Toggle Pixel Aspect Ratio Correction button at the bottom of the Menu Editor window to see an approximation of the menu's appearance on the final DVD.

3 Choose View > Show Selected Subpicture.

The subpictures appear.

4 Choose View > Show Safe Area.

Adobe Encore DVD displays the Title Safe area guides. The title and buttons may be partially outside of the safe viewing area.

5 Using the selection tool, move the Animal Facts text block so that it is positioned completely within the safe viewing area. Then move the three buttons within the safe viewing area, as shown below.

You can edit the menu in Adobe Encore DVD because all of the Photoshop layer information has been preserved.

Editing a menu in Photoshop

The Outer Glow layer style helps to define the shape of the giraffe, but the image still seems to lack contrast. You can add contrast by adjusting the image levels in Photoshop. You can easily edit the menu in Photoshop without losing the changes you've made in Adobe Encore DVD.

1 In Adobe Encore DVD, choose Menu > Edit in Photoshop.

Note: To launch Photoshop from Adobe Encore DVD, Adobe Encore DVD and Photoshop must be installed on the same computer.

Photoshop starts and opens the menu you have just been working on. The menu retains the changes you made in Adobe Encore DVD.

Note: If you are prompted to update the text layers, click Update.

Notice that the filename at the top of the image window is longer than the name of the menu file you created in Photoshop. When you use the Edit in Photoshop command, Adobe Encore DVD creates a copy of the current menu file, gives it a unique name, and stores it in the Sources\Menus folder in the Adobe Encore DVD project folder. Changes you make to this file in Photoshop affect the menu in your Adobe Encore DVD project, but do not affect the original menu file.

2 If the giraffe subpicture layer in the menu is visible in Photoshop, hide it by clicking the eye icon in the Layers palette.

You want to add contrast to the giraffe image, so you need to be able to see the image as it normally appears. Hiding the subpicture layer in Photoshop has no effect in Adobe Encore DVD. Adobe Encore DVD interprets the subpicture layer whether it is visible or hidden.

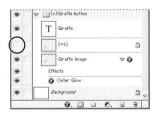

3 Select the Giraffe image layer in the Layers palette

Make sure you select the Giraffe image layer and not the Giraffe text layer, the (+) Giraffe Button layer set, or the (=1) subpicture layer.

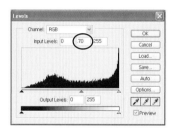

4 Choose Image > Adjustments > Levels.

5 Drag the middle triangle under the histogram slightly to the right. As you drag, the midtones value for the Input Levels changes. We moved the midtones value to .70. Click OK to apply the change.

The giraffe image has better contrast.

6 Save the file in Photoshop, and then close it. Return to Adobe Encore DVD.

In Adobe Encore DVD, the menu has updated to reflect the change you made in Photoshop.

Note: If the subpictures are visible, choose View > Show Selected Subpicture to hide them.

7 Choose File > Save. Name the project **Lesson_03.ncor**.

Linking buttons to timelines

Adobe Encore DVD recognizes the buttons you created in Photoshop, so you can link them just as you would buttons you create in Adobe Encore DVD. First, create the timelines, and then link the buttons.

1 Click the Project window to make it active. Choose File > Import as Asset. In the Import as Asset dialog box, navigate to the Lesson 03 folder. Select **Giraffe.avi, Gorilla.avi,** and **Jaguar.avi.** (Press the Ctrl key to select multiple files.) Click Open.

2 In the Project window, select Giraffe.avi, Gorilla.avi, and Jaguar.avi. Click the Create a New Timeline button at the bottom of the Project window.

The Timeline window opens with three tabs, one for each video file. The Monitor window also opens.

3 If the Properties palette isn't open, choose Window > Properties.

4 In the Project window, select the Giraffe timeline, the Gorilla timeline, and the Jaguar timeline.

5 In the Properties palette, choose Main > Default from the End Action pop-up menu.

Now, after each movie plays, the main menu will appear with its default button highlighted.

6 In the Project window, make sure that the Main menu is set to play when the disc is inserted. (A circle with an arrow ( ) should appear on its icon. If it doesn't, right-click the Main menu and choose File > Set as First Play.)

7 With the selection tool, right-click the Giraffe button in the Menu Editor window, and choose Link To. Select the Giraffe timeline, and click OK.

8 Using the same procedure you used in step 7, link the Gorilla button to the Gorilla timeline, and the Jaguar button to the Jaguar timeline.

9 Save the file.

Repositioning overlapping objects

The buttons have large bounding boxes, so they're probably overlapping. You'll preview the buttons and their subpictures, and then reposition them if they overlap.

1 Choose File > Preview.

The Main menu appears.

2 Mouse over the buttons in the Project Preview window to display their subpictures.

If the bounding boxes for the buttons overlap, the subpictures may not appear as expected. An example is shown below.

3 Close the Project Preview window.

4 Press the Shift key, and click the three buttons in the Menu Editor window.

Notice that even though the buttons are irregularly shaped, they have rectangular bounding boxes. It is easy to accidentally overlap buttons.

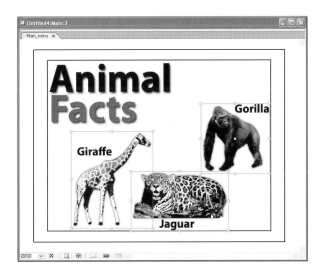

5 Use the selection tool to move the buttons so they do not overlap. Keep them within the Title Safe area.

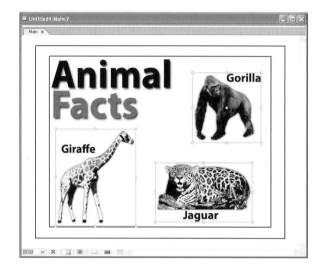

6 Save the file.

Previewing the project

Before you burn a DVD, make sure the project is configured properly. It should look and behave just like the one you previewed at the beginning of this lesson.

1 Choose File > Preview.

If the project is configured correctly, the Main menu appears. The Giraffe button is highlighted.

2 Click the Giraffe button. The Giraffe timeline should play, and then the DVD should return to the main menu.

3 Click the other two buttons. The timelines should play, and then the DVD should return to the main menu.

4 Close the Project Preview window.

If the DVD project didn't behave as described above, return to the project and correct the behavior. Preview the DVD again to ensure that it behaves as expected before continuing.

Burning the DVD

You're ready to burn the DVD.

1 Choose File > Build DVD > Make DVD Disc.

2 In the Make DVD Disc dialog box, choose Current Project from the Create Using pop-up menu, and then choose your recorder.

3 Insert a blank disc in the recorder, and click Next.

4 Review the information in the Make DVD Disc Summary dialog box. When you are ready to proceed, click Build.

Burning the disc may take several minutes, depending on the DVD recorder, the computer system, and the size of the media.

Review questions

1 What's the advantage of creating a menu in Photoshop rather than in Adobe Encore DVD?

2 How do you apply a layer style to text in Photoshop?

3 Which layer sets will Adobe Encore DVD recognize as buttons?

4 Which layers will Adobe Encore DVD recognize as subpictures?

5 How can you edit an Adobe Encore DVD menu in Photoshop?

Review answers

1 When you create a menu in Photoshop, you have full access to the robust, flexible design features in Photoshop. Adobe Encore DVD retains the Photoshop effects when you import the menu.

2 Select the text layer in the Layers palette, and then either choose Layer > Layer Style > [layer style], or click the Add a Layer Style button at the bottom of the Layers palette and choose a layer style.

3 Adobe Encore DVD recognizes layer sets whose names begin with (+) as buttons.

4 Adobe Encore DVD recognizes layers whose names begin with (=) as subpictures.

5 Select the menu in the Project window, and then choose Menu > Edit in Photoshop.

Lesson 4

4 Using Adobe Encore DVD Templates

To get your project started quickly, use one of the menu templates included with Adobe Encore DVD. You can choose the menu, buttons, and images you want to use from the Library palette, and then customize them to create a unique look.

You can use templates to get a head start on your DVD projects—whether you're using one of the templates included with Adobe Encore DVD or one you created yourself. In this lesson you will learn how to do the following:

- Add menus, buttons, and images to the Library palette.
- View only menus, buttons, or images in the Library palette.
- Specify the default menu.
- Open a menu template.
- Edit the text and buttons in a template.
- Edit the background elements of a template.
- Replace an item using the Library palette.
- Paste items into multiple menus.
- Build a DVD image.

Getting started

In this lesson, you'll create a new Adobe Encore DVD project, using graphic and video files included on the *Adobe Encore DVD Classroom in a Book* DVD. Make sure you know the location of the files you need for Lesson 4. For help, see "Copying the Classroom in a Book files" on page 2.

Viewing the finished Adobe Encore DVD project

To see what you'll be creating, take a look at the finished project.

1 Start Adobe Encore DVD.

2 Choose File > Open Project.

3 In the Open dialog box, navigate to the Lesson 04 folder. Select **Lesson_04_end.ncor,** and then click Open.

4 Choose File > Preview.

The Project Preview window opens, displaying a DVD menu. There are two buttons, and the first button is highlighted.

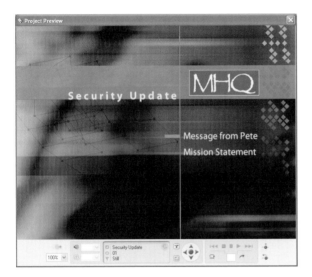

5 Click the Message from Pete button.

A new menu with four buttons appears.

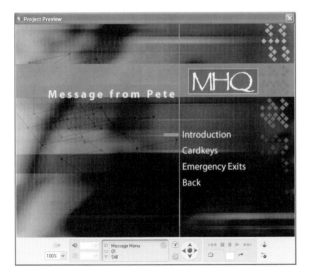

6 Click the Back button to return to the main menu.

7 Click the Mission Statement button. Another menu appears.

8 Close the Project Preview window and the Lesson_04_end Project window.

Exploring the Library palette

You can display the files you want to see in the Library palette, specify default menus and buttons, and perform other tasks.

1 Choose File > New Project. Click OK to accept NTSC as the television standard.

2 Choose Menu > New Menu.

A blank menu appears, with a black background.

3 Choose Window > Layers to open the Layers palette.

Only the Background layer is listed in the Layers palette.

4 Click the Library tab to open the Library palette.

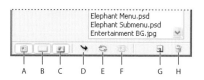

Library palette
*A.Show Menus **B.** Show Buttons **C.**Show Images*
*D. Place **E.** Replace **F.** New Menu **G.** Add Item **H.** Delete*

The first three buttons at the bottom of the Library palette offer different views: the first button shows menus, the second shows buttons, and the third shows images. You can select one, two, all three, or none of the buttons at a time. By default, all three are selected, so all the items in the library are listed.

5 Click the Show Buttons and Show Images buttons to deselect them.

The Library palette lists only the menus in the library. The name of the default menu is preceded by two asterisks (**). The default menu is automatically applied whenever you choose Menu > New Menu or click the New Menu button in the Project window. You can specify which menu is the default menu.

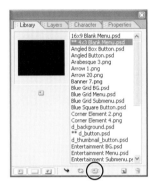

6 Click several different menus. A thumbnail version of the selected menu appears in the preview pane in the Library palette.

You can use these menus as templates, already laid out so that you can simply substitute your text or make any other edits you want to make. The menus are Adobe Photoshop files constructed of layers and layer sets named using Adobe Encore DVD naming conventions.

7 Select the Blue Grid Menu.psd file.

8 Click the New Menu button (▣) at the bottom of the Library palette.

The Blue Grid Menu appears in the Menu Editor window.

When you click the New Menu button in the Library palette, Adobe Encore DVD creates a new menu using the menu file currently selected in the Library palette, rather than the default menu. However, when you choose Menu > New Menu or click the New Menu button in the Project window, Adobe Encore DVD creates a new menu using the default menu.

9 Click the Show Selected Subpicture Highlight button at the bottom of the Menu Editor window. Blue bars appear next to the buttons in the menu.

The subpictures were created in the menu file in Photoshop. In the Layers palette, you can see that the button layer sets include layers whose names begin with (=1).

10 In the Project window, select all the menus you've created, and then delete them.

To delete the selected menus, you can click the Delete button at the bottom of the Project window, or press the Delete key on your keyboard.

Note: Items in the default Adobe Encore DVD library are stored in the Encore DVD 1.0\Library folder on your hard drive. Items you add to the library are stored in the Documents and Settings\<username>\Application Data\Adobe\Adobe Encore DVD\Library folder on your hard drive.

Understanding color sets

A subpicture defines how a button is highlighted when it is selected, activated, or in its normal (unselected) state. The same image is used in each state, but when you vary the colors and opacity, the button can appear quite different in one state than it does in another.

Color sets specify the colors used in subpictures. Each menu can reference only one color set, but you can use many color sets in a project. Typically, using the same color set for all your menus will give your project a consistent look. Each pixel in a subpicture either references one of three colors defined in the color set used for that state, or is transparent. Each state has its own color definitions and opacity settings for all three colors.

For example, using Photoshop, you can create a subpicture composed of three elements, such as a check mark, a button outline, and the button text. Each element references a different color. By adjusting the colors and opacity values, you can have the check mark appear next to a menu button only in the activated state. To do this, you would make the check mark the sole item in the subpicture to use a particular color, such as color 3. Then you could define color 3 as transparent for all but the activated state.

Adobe Encore DVD includes a predefined color set. You can modify the default set or create your own sets. You can save sets and use them in other projects.

In the Blue Grid Menu.psd file, two colors are used for the subpictures. In the normal state, the blue bars are 100% transparent. In the selected or activated state, the bars are 100% blue. You can see the subpictures in the Layers palette; they are the layers that begin with (=1).

For more information, see "Creating subpictures and color sets" in Adobe Encore DVD Help.

Modifying a menu template

You can quickly create sophisticated menus by modifying one of the many templates included with Adobe Encore DVD.

1 Open the Library palette.

2 Select the Sky Up Menu.psd file.

3 Click the New Menu button at the bottom of the Library palette.

The menu opens. It contains four buttons. However, the menu you're creating requires only two main buttons. You'll delete the buttons you don't need.

4 With the selection tool, select the Languages button and the Behind the Scenes button.

5 Press the Delete key on your keyboard.

The Play Movie and Special Features buttons remain in the menu.

6 Open the Layers palette.

7 Select the Title layer set.

8 With the text tool, select "From the Sky Up" in the Menu Editor window, and type **Security Update**.

9 Use the direct select tool to reposition the text so that it is positioned as shown below.

10 In the Layers palette, expand the Play Movie layer set, and select the text layer (named "play movie").

Note: To expand a layer set, click the triangle next to its name.

11 Use the text tool to change the text in the Menu Editor window to **Message from Pete**.

12 Expand the Special Features layer set in the Layers palette, select the text layer (named "special features"), and change the text in the Menu Editor window to **Mission Statement**.

13 If the Properties palette isn't open, choose Window > Properties.

14 With the selection tool, select the first button in the Menu Editor window. In the Properties palette, rename the button **Message**.

Give menus, buttons, and timelines appropriate names to help you organize your project, and to prevent confusion as your project becomes more complex.

15 In the Properties palette, rename the second button **Mission**.

16 Select the menu in the Project window. In the Properties palette, rename it **Security Update**.

The menu's name is automatically updated in the Project window.

17 Ensure that the Security Update menu will play when the DVD is started. It should have a small black triangle next to its name (▲), and "First Play" should appear next to the thumbnail preview in the Project window. If the menu isn't set to play first, right-click it and choose Set as First Play.

18 Save the project. Name it **Lesson_04.ncor**.

Creating submenus from the same template

To create a consistent look for your DVD project, you can use the same template to create all its menus. You'll start with the same template, but you'll make different changes to it.

1 Select the Sky Up Menu.psd file in the Library palette.

2 Click the New Menu button at the bottom of the Library palette.

The Sky Up Menu template opens in the Menu Editor window, just as it did earlier. Changes you make to the menu after you add it to your project do not affect the menu file stored in the library.

3 In the Properties palette, rename the menu **Message**.

4 Expand the Title layer set in the Layers palette, and select the text layer. Then, in the Menu Editor window, use the text tool to change the menu title to **Message**.

5 Use the direct select tool to reposition the title.

6 Replace the text for the first three buttons with **Introduction**, **Cardkeys**, and **Emergency Exits**.

You can select the text and replace it in the Menu Editor window without selecting the text layer in the Layers palette. However, it's easy to accidentally create a new empty text block if you click the text tool outside the text object. Expand the layer set in the Layers palette to ensure that you haven't created extra text layers.

7 Change the text in the Behind the Scenes button to **Back**.

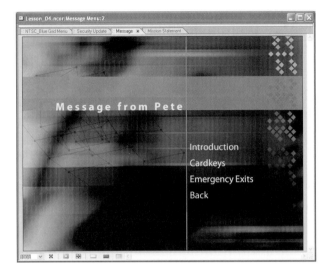

8 With the selection tool, select the first button in the Menu Editor window. In the Properties palette rename the button **Introduction**.

9 Select the other buttons and rename them in the Properties palette, according to each button's name.

10 Save the project.

Replacing background elements

You can edit all aspects of a menu you create from a template, including elements in the background. For example, you can add images or buttons from the Library palette. For this menu, you'll create another submenu from the same template, deleting the buttons and replacing them with an image.

1 Select the Sky Up Menu.psd file in the Library palette, and click the New Menu button.

2 In the Properties palette, rename the menu **Mission Statement**.

3 In the Menu Editor window, use the text tool to change the title to **Mission Statement**.

4 Delete the first three buttons in the Menu Editor window.

This submenu will not link to any other menus or timelines. The only button on the menu will return viewers to the main menu.

5 Change "behind the scenes" to **Back**.

6 Select the Back button with the selection tool in the Menu Editor window, and rename it **Back** in the Properties palette.

7 Expand the Background Details layer set in the Layers palette, and then select the Background layer.

8 Select the Blue Grid BG.psd file in the Library palette.

9 With the Background layer still selected in the Layers palette, click the Replace button (⟳) at the bottom of the Library palette.

The blue-green background image is replaced with a new image.

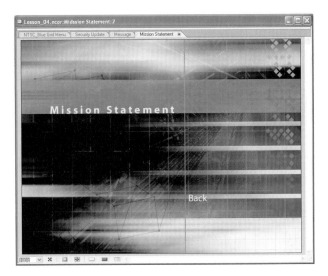

10 Save the project.

Adding items to the Library palette

You can store items you use frequently in the Library palette. Additionally, you can easily position common elements (such as a company logo) in multiple menus.

Add the MHQ company logos to the Library palette for use in this project.

1 Click the Add Item button ( ) at the bottom of the Library palette.

The New Library Item dialog box appears.

2 Select the **MHQ_logo.psd** and **MHQ_logo_white.psd** files. (Press the Ctrl key to select multiple files.) Click Open.

Both logo files appear in the Library palette.

3 Click the Security Update tab in the Menu Editor window.

4 Select the MHQ_logo_white.psd file in the Library palette, and click the Place button (↘) at the bottom of the Library palette.

The Place button adds the selected item to the active menu.

5 Click the Show Safe Area button at the bottom of the Menu Editor window.

Lines appear in the window designating the safe viewing area. You can be sure that anything within this area will appear on all televisions and computer monitors, but some viewers won't see items outside the safe area.

6 With the selection tool, position the logo in the upper-right area of the menu. Keep the logo within the safe area.

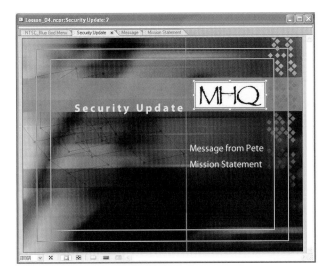

The logo color doesn't work well in this menu, so you will replace the logo with a different version.

7 Select the MHQ_logo.psd file in the Library palette.

8 Make sure the original logo is still selected in the Menu Editor window, and then click the Replace button at the bottom of the Library palette.

The first logo has been replaced by the second, and appears in the same position.

9 With the logo still selected in the Menu Editor window, choose Edit > Copy.

10 Click the Message tab at the top of the Menu Editor window.

11 Choose Edit > Paste.

The logo is pasted into the same location it occupies in the Security Update menu.

12 Paste the logo into the same position in the Mission Statement menu.

Once you've positioned an item in one menu, you can quickly add it to other menus in the same position.

13 Save the project.

Linking menus to each other

Link the menus to each other, just as you would if you created them from scratch, or if you imported them as menus.

1 Click the Security Update tab in the Menu Editor window, and then select the Message from Pete button.

2 In the Properties palette, choose Message > Introduction from the Link pop-up menu.

3 Select the Mission Statement button, and in the Properties palette, link the button to Mission Statement > Back.

4 Now click the Mission Statement tab in the Menu Editor window to open the Mission Statement menu.

5 Select the Back button, and in the Properties palette, link the button to Security Update > Message.

6 Save the project.

Linking buttons to timelines

You will link the buttons in the Message menu to timelines. First, you'll import the video files.

1 Click in the Project window to make it active. Choose File > Import as Asset. In the Import as Asset dialog box, navigate to the Lesson 04 folder. Press the Ctrl key as you select the **Cardkey.avi, Exits.avi**, and **Intro.avi** files. Click Open.

2 In the Project window, select the Cardkey.avi, Exits.avi, and Intro.avi files, and choose Timeline > New Timeline.

The three video assets are placed in timelines, and the Monitor window opens.

3 Click the Message tab in the Menu Editor window, and then select the Introduction button.

4 In the Properties palette, choose Intro > Chapter 1 from the Link pop-up menu.

5 Repeat steps 3 and 4 for the Cardkey button and the Emergency Exit button, linking the buttons to their respective timelines.

6 Save the project.

Creating a text layer

You can create a menu that contains a message. For this project, you'll add text to the Mission Statement menu.

1 Click the Mission Statement tab in the Menu Editor window.

2 With the text tool, drag to create a box in the bottom-left area of the menu.

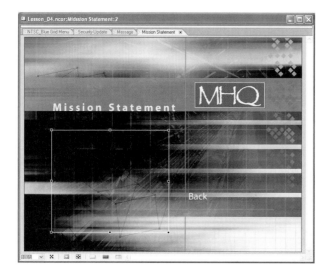

3 In the Character palette, choose Myriad Pro for the font, Bold Condensed for the font style, 48 for the type size, and white for the color. (Select NTSC Colors Only.) Click the Align Center option.

4 With the text tool, click inside the box you just created. Type the following words:

To provide a safe and healthy work environment.

Use the selection tool to position the text block.

5 Save the project.

Checking links

This project has three linking menus and three timelines, and the number of links has grown. It is easy to miss unlinked buttons and menus. Tabs in the Project window help you organize your assets and see how they are linked.

1 In the Project window, click the Menus tab.

The Menus tab lists only the menus included in the project. It does not list timelines, video clips, or other assets.

2 Click the Message menu. If necessary, stretch the window so that you can see the settings fields.

The Link field identifies the link for each button in the selected menu. Notice that no link has been set for the Back button.

3 In the lower frame of the Menus tab, select the Back button. In the Properties palette, choose Security Update > Default from the Link pop-up menu.

4 Click the other menus to check for unlinked buttons.

5 Click the Timelines tab in the Project window.

The end action is listed for each timeline.

6 Select all three timelines. In the Properties palette, choose Message: Default from the End Action pop-up menu.

7 When you have confirmed that all buttons are linked and all timelines have end actions assigned, save the project.

Previewing the project

Preview the project to make sure that the menus are consistent, and that the links behave as you expect them to.

1 Choose File > Preview to open the Project Preview window.

2 Click the Message from Pete button to open the Message menu. Click the buttons to view the three timelines, and then click the Back button to return to the Security Update menu.

3 Click the Mission Statement button to open the Mission Statement menu. Then click Back to return to the Security Update menu.

4 Close the Project Preview window.

Building a DVD image

Your project is finished. Instead of burning the files to disc, you'll build a DVD image. A DVD image can be used to burn a DVD at a different time, or using a remote recorder, such as one at a replication facility.

Note: Adobe Encore DVD also supports the DLT format, which many replication facilities require.

1 Choose File > Build DVD > Make DVD Image.

2 Choose Current Project from the Create Using pop-up menu.

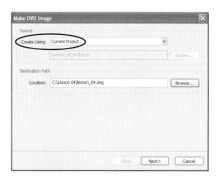

3 Specify a destination for the DVD image, and click Next.

💡 *Ensure that there is sufficient space on the drive you specify.*

4 Review the information in the Make DVD Image: Summary dialog box.

5 Click Build.

Burning a DVD from a DVD image file

You can use Adobe Encore DVD to burn an image file created by Adobe Encore DVD without having access to the original source materials, or even the Adobe Encore DVD project file. The image file contains all the information needed to burn the disc.

1 If the Lesson_04 project is still open, save and close the project.

2 With no projects open in Encore DVD, choose File > Build DVD > Make DVD Disc.

3 Choose Disc Image from the Create Using pop-up menu.

4 Click the Browse button and navigate to the disc image you just created, and click Open.

5 In the Make DVD Disc dialog box, click Next.

6 Review the information in the Make DVD Image: Summary dialog box.

7 Click Build.

Review questions

1 How can you add an item to the Library palette?

2 What can you store in the Library palette?

3 What is the default menu?

4 How can you customize a template?

5 How can you replace an item in a menu with an item from the Library palette?

Review answers

1 Click the New Library Item button at the bottom of the Library palette, and then select the item you want to add in the New Library Item dialog box.

2 You can store background images, buttons, other images, and menus that you want to use as templates in the Library palette, for quick and easy access from any project.

3 The default menu is the menu that Adobe Encore DVD opens when you choose Menu > New Menu or click the New Menu button at the bottom of the Project window.

4 To customize a template, edit it as you would any other menu you've created in Adobe Encore DVD. Once you've created an initial menu from a template, it is fully editable.

5 To replace an item, first select it in the Menu Editor window. Then select the replacement item in the Library palette, and click the Replace button.

Lesson 5

5 Assembling a DVD Quickly

Sometimes you just need to provide a convenient way to view rough video clips. When speed is your priority, use the shortcut features built into Adobe Encore DVD to streamline your workflow.

As you've seen in previous lessons, you can create elegant navigation schemes for a DVD using Adobe Encore DVD. For some projects, however, the speed with which you can create the DVD is more important than the style of the DVD. In this lesson, you'll create a DVD from rough clips, using productivity features in Adobe Encore DVD to accomplish tasks quickly.

In the last lesson, you used menu templates from the Library palette. In this lesson, you will use the Library palette more extensively, and create a DVD with a minimal number of steps. In the process, you will learn how to do the following:

• Set the default menu in the Library palette.

• Set the default button in the Library palette.

• Import items directly into the Library palette.

• Simultaneously create buttons and timelines, and links between them.

• Arrange, resize, and position buttons in a menu.

• Add data files to a disc.

• Burn a CD using Adobe Encore DVD.

Getting started

In this lesson, you'll quickly assemble an Adobe Encore DVD project, using graphic and video files included on the *Adobe Encore DVD Classroom in a Book* DVD. Make sure you know the location of the files you need for Lesson 5. For help, see "Copying the Classroom in a Book files" on page 2.

Viewing the finished Adobe Encore DVD project

To see what you'll be creating, take a look at the finished project.

1 Start Adobe Encore DVD.

2 Choose File > Open Project.

3 In the Open dialog box, navigate to the Lesson 05 folder. Select **Lesson_05_end.ncor**, and then click Open.

4 Choose File > Preview.

The Project Preview window opens, displaying a DVD menu. There are three buttons, and the first button is highlighted.

5 Click the Dibble St. button.

A raw video clip plays. When the video finishes, the main menu reappears.

6 Click each of the other buttons to view the other video clips.

7 Close the Project Preview window and the Lesson_05_end Project window.

Dragging items into the Library palette

Adobe Encore DVD includes several menus, buttons, and images in its Library palette. You can add your own assets to the Library palette, simply by dragging them there. Because you can use items in the Library palette in any project, it's a good idea to add your standard corporate menu templates, company logos, and any other items you use frequently.

When you create a new menu, Adobe Encore DVD automatically uses the menu that is currently set as the default menu in the Library palette.

1 Choose File > New Project. Click OK to accept NTSC as the television standard.

2 Open the Library palette.

If the palette is already open, click its tab to make it active. If it isn't open, choose Window > Library to open it.

3 Deselect the Show Buttons and Show Images buttons at the bottom of the Library palette.

By default, the Library palette lists all the menus, buttons, and images in the library. When you deselect the Show Buttons and Show Images buttons, only the menus are displayed.

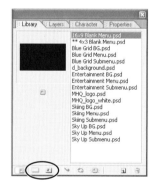

Notice that one of the menu names is preceded by two asterisks. The asterisks indicate the current default menu.

4 Choose File > Import as Menu.

5 Navigate to the Lesson 05 folder. Select **Capstan Main.psd,** and click Open.

The Capstan Main menu appears in the Menu Editor window. This menu does not contain any buttons or editable text layers. You will add those later. The file is listed in the Project window, where it is available for this project. To make this menu available for future projects, you will add it to the Library palette.

6 Drag the Capstan Main.psd file from the Project window to the Library palette.

Capstan Main.psd is listed in the Library palette. It will remain in the Library palette when you work on future projects, unless you delete it.

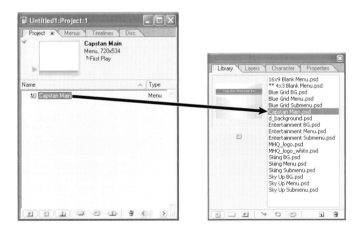

7 Right-click the Capstan Main.psd file in the Library palette, and choose Set as Default Menu.

Two asterisks appear in front of the menu name, changing it to **Capstan Main.psd.

Now if you chose Menu > New Menu, Adobe Encore DVD would create a new menu using the Capstan Main.psd file.

8 Save the project. Name it **Lesson_05.ncor.**

Importing items into the Library palette

You can also add items to the Library palette without first adding them to your project. As with the default menu, you can also set a default button in the Library palette, which is the button Adobe Encore DVD uses when you create a new button.

1 In the Library palette, deselect the Show Menus button, and then select the Show Buttons button.

Only buttons are listed in the Library palette.

2 Click the Add Item button at the bottom of the Library palette.

3 Navigate to the Lesson 05 folder, and select **Capstan Button.psd**. Then click Open.

Capstan Button.psd is listed in the Library palette. The new button is selected, and a thumbnail of the button appears in the Library palette.

4 Right-click the Capstan Button.psd file in the Library palette, and choose Set as Default Button.

Two asterisks appear before Capstan Button.psd, changing its name to **Capstan Button.psd.

Creating buttons instantly

When the structure of your DVD is straightforward, you can combine steps to quickly create a timeline, a corresponding button, and a link between the two. Just drag the video asset directly onto the Menu Editor window to make it all happen.

1 Choose File > Import as Asset.

If Import as Asset is dimmed, click the Project window to make it active, and then choose File > Import as Asset.

2 Navigate to the Lesson 05 folder. Select **Dibble.avi**, **Pine.avi**, and **Stewart.avi** in the Lesson 05 folder, and then click Open. Press the Ctrl key to select multiple files.

The files appear in the Project window.

3 Drag the Dibble.avi file from the Project window onto the Menu Editor window.

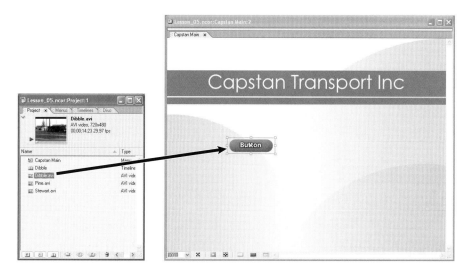

Adobe Encore DVD performed several tasks when you dragged the video asset onto the Menu Editor window:

• The default button appears in the menu.

• A new timeline was created for the video asset.

• The button was linked to the new timeline. When you play or preview the DVD, activating the button will play the linked timeline.

• The End Action field for the timeline has been set to return to the menu.

• The Menu Remote field for the timeline has been set to return to the menu.

4 Drag the Pine.avi and Stewart.avi assets onto the Menu Editor window. To select them both, press the Ctrl key as you select them, and then release it before you drag them.

Adobe Encore DVD performs all of the tasks listed above for these video assets as well. This project is almost finished!

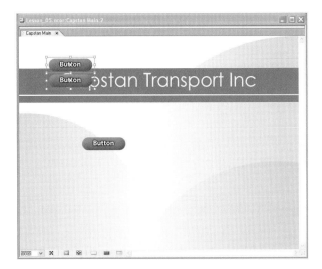

5 Save the project.

Resizing and positioning buttons

When you dragged the video assets to the Menu Editor window, Adobe Encore DVD created the buttons wherever you dropped the assets. You'll position them exactly where you want them. Additionally, the buttons are a little too small for this menu, so you'll resize them.

1 Using the selection tool, select the three buttons in the Menu Editor window. (They may already be selected.) Press the Shift key to select all three.

2 Move the cursor to a corner handle on one of the buttons. The cursor turns into a diagonal double arrow (↖).

3 Hold down the Shift key, and drag the corner handle away from the center to enlarge the buttons. Holding down the Shift key constrains the proportions of the buttons.

By resizing all three buttons at once, you can be sure that the final buttons are the same size. Now reposition the buttons.

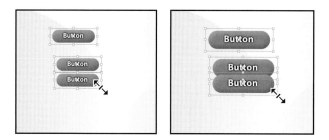

4 Click the Show Safe Area button at the bottom of the Menu Editor window to display the Title Safe area guides.

Anything within the guides will appear on a television screen; anything outside the guides may not.

5 Drag each of the buttons to the right side of the menu, within the safe area.

It doesn't matter which order the buttons are in.

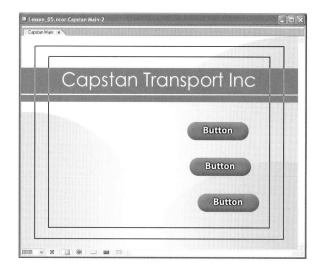

6 With the buttons positioned roughly as shown, select all three buttons in the Menu Editor window, and choose Object > Align > Left.

The left sides of the button align with the left side of the first button you selected.

7 With the buttons still selected, choose Object > Distribute > Vertically.

The same amount of space appears between the first and second button as between the second and third buttons.

8 Save the project.

Editing button text

The text of each button currently reads "Button." You need to change the text for each button to refer to the timeline it links to.

1 Open the Properties palette, if it isn't open.

2 Using the selection tool, select the top button in the Menu Editor window.

3 Note the timeline displayed in the Link field in the Properties palette.

4 With the text tool, select the word "Button" on the top button, and type the name of the street shown in the Link field of the Properties palette.

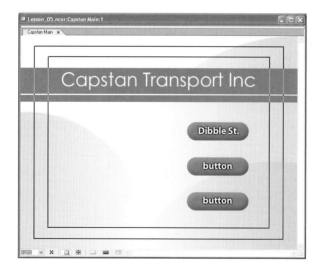

In the illustration, Dibble St. is the top button. If your buttons are arranged differently, the top button in your menu may link to a different timeline. Name the button to correspond with its link.

5 If necessary, use the direct select tool to select just the text block of the button, and reposition it so it is centered within the button.

6 Repeat steps 2-5 for the other two buttons, naming the buttons to refer to the linked timelines as shown in the Properties palette.

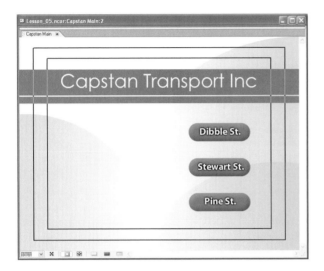

7 Save the project.

Adding a title to the menu

The menu contains a company name, but no title. You'll add a title to the menu to help the viewer understand the contents of the DVD.

1 Drag the text tool to create a rectangle in the left side of the menu between the Title Safe area guides and the buttons.

2 Open the Character palette. Choose Myriad Pro for the font, Bold for the font style, 36 for the type size, and black for the color. (Select NTSC Colors Only in the Color Picker.) Click the Align Left option.

3 Type **Potential Sites for the Proposed Distribution Center.**

4 Use the selection tool to position the text block you just created.

5 Save the project.

Previewing the project

You can preview the project at any stage, but it's particularly important to preview the project before you burn it to disc.

1 Choose File > Preview to open the Project Preview window.

2 Click any button to play the appropriate video. The timeline should play and then return to the main menu.

3 Click the Remote Control Title Button and Remote Control Menu Button buttons while the timelines are playing.

4 When you are done, close the Project Preview window.

Adding data files to a disc

You can add a folder of data files to a disc, in addition to the content you've configured using Adobe Encore DVD. For this project, you'll include an Adobe PDF file of a map that shows the location of each of the proposed sites.

1 Click the Disc tab in the Project window.

2 Click Browse in the DVD Content section of the Disc tab. Navigate to the Lesson 05 folder, and select the Map folder. Click OK.

Note: Data files you add to a DVD are not accessible through menus or buttons on the DVD. To access those files on a DVD, view the contents of the disc in Windows Explorer.

Burning a CD

Instead of burning this project onto a DVD, you'll burn it onto a blank CD-ROM. CDs created in Adobe Encore DVD play only in computer-based DVD-compatible drives. The capacity of a CD is typically 650-700 MB, significantly less than that of a DVD. However, when you're distributing small projects that are not intended for television viewing, you may prefer to write DVD-compliant files to a CD. The quality will equal that of a DVD.

1 In the Disc tab, choose 650 MB or 700 MB from the disc size pop-up menu, depending on the capacity of your blank CD.

2 Click Build Project. If prompted to save your project, click Save and Continue.

3 In the Make DVD Disc dialog box, choose Current Project from the Create Using pop-up menu, and then choose your recorder.

4 Insert a blank CD in the recorder, and click Next.

5 Click Build in the Make DVD Disc Summary dialog box.

Burning the disc may take several minutes, depending on the recorder, the computer system, and the size of the media.

Review questions

1 Name two ways to add an item to the Library palette.

2 How can you set a default menu?

3 What happens when you drag a video asset onto the Menu Editor window?

4 How can you ensure that you resize buttons on a menu consistently?

5 How can you align buttons with each other?

Review answers

1 You can drag an asset from the Project window to the Library palette. Alternatively, you can click the Add Item button in the Library palette, and then select the file you want to add.

2 Right-click the menu in the Library palette, and choose Set as Default Menu from the context menu.

3 Adobe Encore DVD performs several tasks when you drag a video asset onto the Menu Editor window:

- A timeline is created for the video asset.

- A new button is created, using the default button in the Library palette.

- The button is linked to the timeline.

- The End Action field for the timeline is set to return to the menu.

- The Menu Remote field for the timeline is set to return to the menu.

4 Select the buttons you want to resize, and then drag a corner handle. All the buttons resize at once.

5 Select the buttons you want to align and choose Object > Align, and choose the side along which you want to align them. The buttons are aligned with the position of the first button you select.

Lesson 6

6 | Overriding Default Actions

Each timeline has a default end action assigned. For greater flexibility, Adobe Encore DVD lets you override that default end action when the timeline is accessed in different ways.

In this lesson, you'll create a DVD with three video clips, which can be viewed in sequence or individually. You will use two linked menus to provide the navigation. As you work on this DVD project, you will learn how to do the following:

- Work with multiple menus.
- Set default end actions so that timelines play in sequence.
- Link menus to each other.
- Use the pick whip to create links visually.
- Use the override feature to provide alternative end action behaviors.
- Use the Menus tab of the Project window.
- Make a DVD folder.

Getting started

In previous lessons, you've linked menus to timelines, set end actions to determine what happens when a timeline has played, and specified a First Play action. Many DVD projects include multiple menus that link to the same timelines; you may not want the timeline's behavior to be the same each time. Adobe Encore DVD lets you specify overrides when the default action is not appropriate.

In this lesson, you'll create a more complex Adobe Encore DVD project, using graphic and video files included on the *Adobe Encore DVD Classroom in a Book* DVD. Make sure you know the location of the files you need for Lesson 6. For help, see "Copying the Classroom in a Book files" on page 2.

Viewing the finished Adobe Encore DVD project

To see what you'll be creating, take a look at the finished project.

1 Start Adobe Encore DVD.

2 Choose File > Open Project.

3 In the Open dialog box, navigate to the Lesson 06 folder. Select **Lesson_06_end.ncor**, and then click Open.

4 Choose File > Preview.

The Project Preview window opens, displaying a DVD menu. There are two buttons, and the default button is highlighted.

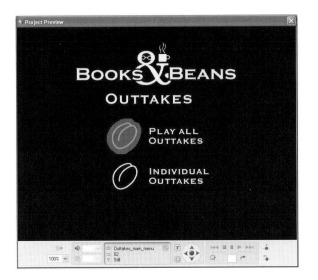

5 Click the Play All Outtakes button.

Three videos play in sequence. After each video has finished playing, the next video plays automatically. After the third video plays, the main menu reappears.

6 Click the Individual Outtakes button.

A new menu named "Individual Outtakes" appears. It contains three named buttons and a Back button.

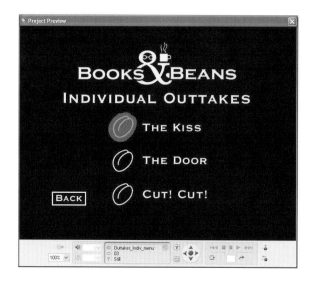

7 Click each of the named buttons to play an individual timeline.

After each video plays, the Individual Outtakes menu reappears.

8 Click the Back button to return to the main menu.

9 Close the Project Preview window and the Lesson_06_end Project window.

About overrides

An end action determines what happens when a timeline or motion menu finishes playing. You can set only one end action for each timeline or menu, but you may want a timeline or menu to behave differently depending on the way it was accessed. For example, in this lesson, you want all three videos to play in sequence when the Play All Outtakes button is selected, so you'll set the end action for each timeline to play the next timeline. However, you want to play only one video at a time when a scene is selected from the Individual Outtakes menu. To make this possible, you'll set an override for each timeline. When a button on the Individual Outtakes menu is selected, Adobe Encore DVD honors the override instead of the default end action for the timeline.

Working with multiple menus

This DVD project includes two menus and three video timelines. To begin the project, you'll define the end actions for the timelines, so that they play sequentially.

1 Choose File > New Project. Click OK to accept NTSC as the television standard.

The Project window opens. Next you'll import the menus.

2 Right-click in the Project window, and choose Import as Menu. Navigate to the Lesson 06 folder. Select the **Outtakes_main.psd** and **Outtakes_Indiv.psd** files, and then click Open. (To select multiple files, hold down the Ctrl key.)

These files were created in Adobe Photoshop, using layers that are named according to Adobe Encore DVD naming conventions. Adobe Encore DVD automatically converts the files to menus, and converts the layers to buttons and subpictures, as appropriate.

When you import a menu into the Project window, Adobe Encore DVD opens the Menu Editor window and displays the menu. When you import two menus, both are open in the Menu Editor window. Adobe Encore DVD displays a tab for each one. You can have several menus open in the Menu Editor window at once.

3 Click the Outtakes_main tab in the Menu Editor window to view the main menu.

This menu has two buttons. One button, named "Play All Outtakes," will play the three timelines in sequence. The other button, named "Individual Outtakes," will link to the Outtakes_Indiv menu.

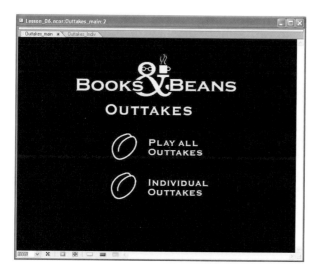

4 Click the Outtakes_Indiv tab in the Menu Editor window to view the second menu.

This menu has four buttons. Three will link to the individual timelines, and one will link back to the main menu.

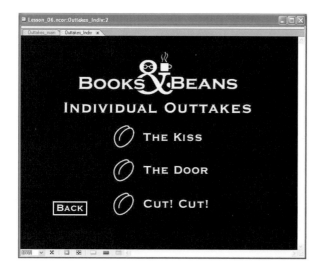

5 In the Project window, make sure that the Outtakes_main menu is set for First Play. A small black triangle appears next to the name of the item set for first play in the Project window. If the Outtakes_main menu isn't designated for First Play, right-click it and choose Set as First Play.

6 Choose File > Save As, and name the project **Lesson_06.ncor**.

Setting default end actions

You will set a default end action for each timeline. The default end action determines what happens when the timeline ends if no override is specified.

1 Right-click in the Project window, and choose Import as Asset. Navigate to the Lesson 06 folder. Select **Cut.avi**, **Door.avi**, and **Kiss.avi**, and then click Open.

You can preview a video asset in the Project window. When you select the video file, a thumbnail of the file appears at the top of the window. Click the Play button next to the thumbnail to play the video.

2 In the Project window, select all three of the AVI files you just imported. Click the Create a New Timeline button at the bottom of the Project window.

The Timeline window opens with three tabs, one for each video file. Adobe Encore DVD has placed each video file into its own timeline, and named it to match the original AVI filename. The Monitor window opens as well.

3 In the Project window, select the Kiss timeline.

Note: Make sure you select the timeline rather than the AVI file.

4 Choose Window > Properties to open the Properties palette, if it isn't already open. It displays the properties for the Kiss timeline.

5 In the Properties palette, choose Door > Chapter 1 from the End Action pop-up menu.

By default, when the Kiss timeline ends, the Door timeline will play.

6 Select the Door timeline in the Project window.

The Properties palette displays the properties for the Door timeline.

7 In the Properties palette, choose Cut > Chapter 1 from the End Action pop-up menu.

By default, when the Door timeline ends, the Cut timeline will play.

8 Finally, select the Cut timeline in the Project window. Then, in the Properties palette, choose Outtakes_main > Default from the End Action pop-up menu.

By default, when the Cut timeline ends, the Outtakes_main menu appears with the Play All Outtakes button highlighted.

Setting links for the main menu

Adobe Encore DVD recognizes buttons in the Photoshop files you imported as layers, but the buttons aren't linked to anything yet. You'll link the buttons in the main menu first.

1 Click the Outtakes_main tab in the Menu Editor window.

2 With the selection tool, right-click the Play All Outtakes button in the Menu Editor window, and then choose Link To.

The Specify Link dialog box opens.

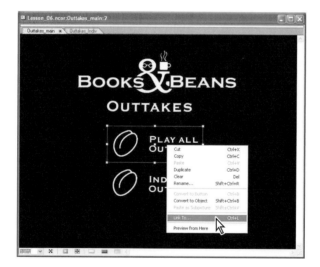

3 Select Kiss, and click OK.

You only need to link the button to the Kiss timeline. The end actions you set in the previous section ensure that after the Kiss timeline plays, the Door timeline will play, and when it finishes, the Cut timeline will automatically play.

Notice that the Target field in the Specify Link dialog box reads Kiss > Chapter 1. Because the Kiss timeline has only one chapter point, selecting the timeline automatically selects the first chapter. If a timeline includes multiple chapters, click the arrow to the left of the timeline's name to display them. You may then select a specific chapter.

4 With the selection tool, right-click the Individual Outtakes button in the Menu Editor window, and choose Link To.

5 In the Specify Link dialog box, click the arrow to the left of Outtakes_Indiv. Select The Kiss, and click OK.

Just as you can display a timeline's chapters in the Specify Link dialog box, you can display a menu's buttons. You have set the link for the Individual Outtakes button so that when it is activated, the Outtakes_Indiv menu will appear, with the The Kiss button highlighted.

6 Save the project.

Previewing the links

You can preview an unfinished project. Though you haven't set all the links and behaviors for this project yet, you'll preview the links from the Outtakes_main menu before moving on to link the buttons in the next menu.

Note: The Preview feature works only if a menu or timeline has been set as First Play.

1 Choose File > Preview.

2 Click the Play All Outtakes button.

All three scenes should play in sequence. Then the Outtakes_main menu should reappear, with the Play All Outtakes button selected.

3 Click the Individual Outtakes button.

The Outtakes_Indiv menu appears. You haven't linked its buttons yet, so clicking them has no effect.

4 Close the Project Preview window.

Using the pick whip

So far, you have used two different methods to create links from buttons to menus and timelines: choosing a link destination from the Specify Link dialog box, or from the pop-up menu in the Properties palette. Adobe Encore DVD also offers a more visual way to create links: the pick whip. If you've used the pick whip in Adobe GoLive or Adobe After Effects, the pick whip in Adobe Encore DVD will seem familiar.

You'll start by linking the Back button to the Outtakes_main menu.

1 Click the Outtakes_Indiv tab in the Menu Editor window. If the tab isn't available, double-click the Outtakes_Indiv menu in the Project window.

2 With the selection tool, select the Back button in the Menu Editor window. Ensure that the attributes for the Back button are displayed in the Properties palette.

3 Arrange your screen so that you can see both the Properties palette and the Project window.

4 Click the pick whip icon (⊚) on the left side of the Link field, and drag it to the Outtakes_main menu in the Project window. When a box appears around Outtakes_main, release the mouse button.

As you drag the pick whip, a straight line appears between the Properties palette and the pick whip cursor. When the cursor is over a menu or timeline in the Project window, Adobe Encore DVD displays a box to identify the selected item. After you release the mouse button, the Properties palette displays the link that you created.

5 Save the project.

Setting overrides

Earlier, you set the end actions for the three video timelines so that they will play in sequence. However, when the buttons in this menu are activated, you want each timeline to play separately and then return to the Outtakes_Indiv menu. Therefore, you'll link the buttons to the timelines, and then specify overrides to perform end actions that are different from the timelines' defaults.

1 In the Menu Editor window, use the selection tool to select the The Kiss button. Make sure the Properties palette displays the attributes for the The Kiss button.

2 Arrange your screen so that you can see both the Properties palette and the Project window.

3 Drag the Link pick whip from the Properties palette to the Kiss timeline in the Project window. When the Kiss timeline is selected, release the mouse button.

As you drag over the items in the Project window, notice that the pick whip does not select the AVI files. Only timelines and menus may be linked to buttons. Because the Kiss timeline has only one chapter (marked by the default chapter point at the beginning of the timeline), that chapter is automatically selected.

When you activate the The Kiss button, the Kiss timeline will play. Earlier in this lesson, you set the default end action for the Kiss timeline to play the Door timeline.

However, you want a different end action when you activate this button. The Outtakes_Indiv menu should appear immediately after the Kiss timeline has finished playing. You will create an override to set this behavior.

4 Drag the Override pick whip from the Properties palette to the Outtakes_Indiv menu in the Project window.

The Override field in the Properties palette reads Outtakes_Indiv: Default. When the timeline ends, the Individual Outtakes menu will appear with the default button selected.

However, for this project, you want the button for the next scene to be selected. For example, after you click the The Kiss button, the Kiss timeline plays, and the The Door button is already selected when the menu reappears. To accomplish this, you'll relink the override to a specific button in a menu.

5 In the Project window, click the Menus tab.

The two menus in the project appear in the window.

6 Select the Outtakes_Indiv menu in the Menus tab.

The buttons associated with the Outtakes_Indiv menu appear in the pane below the menus.

7 Select the The Kiss button in the Menu Editor window again. Drag the Override pick whip from the Properties palette to the The Door button in the lower pane of the Menu window.

The Override value in the Properties palette changes from Outtakes_Indiv: Default to Outtakes_Indiv: The Door.

Now you will set the links and overrides for the other two buttons.

8 Click the Timelines tab in the Project window.

The three timelines appear. The tabs in the Project window give you additional ways to sort and organize your project assets.

9 In the Menu Editor window, use the selection tool to select the The Door button. Make sure the Properties palette displays the attributes for the The Door button.

10 Drag the Link pick whip from the Properties palette to the Door timeline in the Project window.

11 In the Project window, click the Menus tab. Click the The Door button in the Menu Editor window to make sure the Properties palette displays the attributes for the The Door button. Drag the Override pick whip to the Cut button in the lower pane of the Menu tab.

12 Repeat steps 8-11 to link the Cut button to the Cut timeline, and set the override to the Back button in the Outtakes_Indiv menu.

13 Save the project.

Previewing the project

Before you burn your DVD, make sure the links and overrides are working as you intend them to. The project should look like the completed project you previewed at the beginning of the lesson.

1 Choose File > Preview.

The Project Preview window opens, and the Outtakes_main menu appears. There are two buttons, and the default button is highlighted.

2 Click the Play All Outtakes button.

Three videos play in sequence. After each video has finished playing, the next video plays automatically. After the third video plays, the main menu reappears.

3 Click the Individual Outtakes button.

A new menu named "Individual Outtakes" appears. It contains four buttons.

4 Click each button to play an individual timeline.

After each video plays, the Outtakes_Indiv menu reappears.

5 Click the Back button.

The main menu reappears.

Close the Project Preview window. If your DVD project did not behave as described, return to the project and correct the links or overrides.

Making a DVD folder

In earlier lessons, you've burned DVD discs and built a DVD image. Now you'll build a DVD folder for this project. When you build a DVD folder, Adobe Encore DVD builds a DVD directory structure on your hard drive so that you can test its quality or play it locally on a personal computer. You can play the program using a software DVD player that supports the DVD folder; the directory behaves just like a disc, providing full navigational abilities.

Note: Some popular media players do not support DVD folders.

1 Choose File > Build DVD > Make DVD Folder.

2 In the Make DVD Folder dialog box, specify a location and name for the folder, and click Next.

Ensure that you have sufficient space on the drive you specify.

3 Review the information in the Make DVD Folder: Summary dialog box, and then click Build.

Review questions

1 How many end actions can you specify for a timeline?

2 When do you need to apply an override?

3 How do you set an override?

4 What three methods have you used to link buttons to timelines and menus?

5 How do you use the pick whip?

Review answers

1 You can specify only one end action for each timeline. This becomes the default behavior.

2 You need to apply an override when you want the end action for a timeline or menu to be different from the default action, depending on the method used to access the timeline or menu. That is, you need to use an override any time one timeline may have different end actions.

3 To set an override, select the button to which it applies, and then use the pick whip or the pop-up menu in the Properties dialog box to set the action.

4 In this and previous lessons, you've linked buttons using the following methods:

• Right-click the button in the Menu Editor window, choose Link To, and then select the destination for the link.

• Select the button in the Menu Editor window, and then choose the destination from the Link pop-up menu in the Properties palette.

• Select the button in the Menu Editor window, and then use the pick whip to select the link's destination.

5 To use the pick whip, click the pick whip icon in the Properties palette and, continuing to hold the mouse button down, drag it to the item you want to select in the Project window.

Lesson 7

Creating Motion Menus

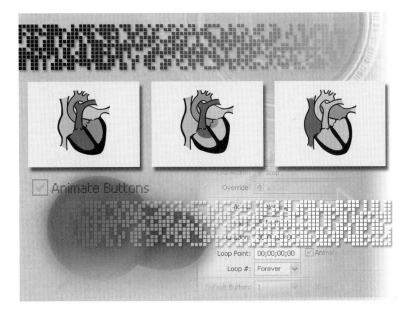

Provide additional cues to viewers, or simply add interest to the project, by using audio or video clips in the background or buttons for your menu. In Adobe Encore DVD, you can also use thumbnails of video clips for buttons, to give viewers a glimpse of what they'll see if they click the button.

In this lesson, you'll create a motion menu, which is a menu that contains an animated background, animated buttons, audio, or a combination of these things. While working on this project, you will learn how to do the following:

- Trim a video in the Timeline window.
- Use different methods to move the current-time indicator in the Timeline window.
- Add video to the background of a menu.
- Render and preview motion menus.
- Transcode an AVI file from the Project window.
- Create thumbnail buttons.
- Specify poster frames for thumbnail buttons.
- Animate thumbnail buttons.

Getting started

In earlier lessons, you created still menus for DVD projects. A motion menu, which includes moving footage or audio, can be more interesting for viewers, especially if the footage or audio provides a hint of what's to come. The audio may be music, sounds, or even someone talking while the menu is displayed. You can create buttons that include thumbnail images of the videos they link to, giving the viewer more information about each video.

In this lesson, you'll create an Adobe Encore DVD project that includes motion menus, using graphic and video files included on the *Adobe Encore DVD Classroom in a Book* DVD. Make sure you know the location of the files you need for Lesson 7. For help, see "Copying the Classroom in a Book files" on page 2.

Viewing the finished Adobe Encore DVD project

To see the motion menus you'll be creating, take a look at the finished project.

1 Start Adobe Encore DVD.

2 Choose File > Open Project.

3 In the Open dialog box, navigate to the Lesson 07 folder. Select **Lesson_07_end.ncor,** and then click Open.

4 Choose File > Preview.

The Project Preview window opens, displaying a DVD menu with a looping video background. There are two buttons, and the first button is selected.

Note: If the background of the menu isn't moving, choose File > Render Motion Menus, and select Preview When Complete.

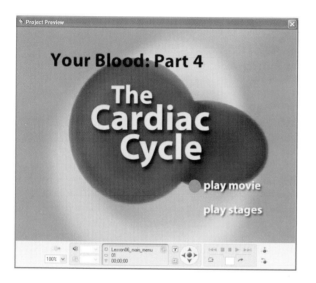

5 Click the Play Movie button.

A video with four sections plays. After the video plays, the initial menu reappears.

6 Click the Play Stages button.

A second menu appears. It contains four buttons with animated thumbnails representing the four sections of the video.

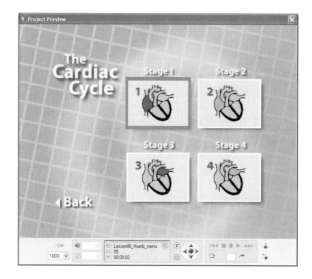

7 Click one or two of the buttons to play the video from that point in the sequence. After each video plays, the thumbnail menu reappears.

8 Close the Project Preview window and the Lesson_07_end Project window.

Assembling your assets

Before you create your motion menu, you will gather the components of your DVD project, and create a timeline for the background.

1 Choose File > New Project. Click OK to accept NTSC as the television standard.

2 Choose File > Import as Menu. Navigate to the Lesson 07 folder. Import the **Cardiac_main.psd** file. This menu file contains several layers and a background layer set.

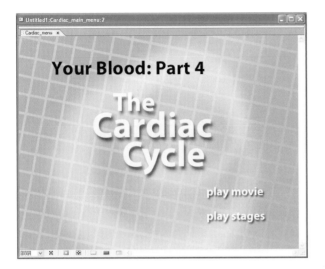

3 Choose File > Import as Asset. Navigate to the Lesson 07 folder. Select the **Cardiac_cycle.avi** file. Click Open.

Note: If the Import as Asset command is dimmed, click the Project window to make it active.

4 In the Project window, select the Cardiac_cycle.avi file.

5 Click the Create a New Timeline button at the bottom of the Project window.

The Timeline window opens with the new Cardiac_cycle timeline active. The Monitor window also opens, displaying the Cardiac_cycle timeline.

6 Play the video in the Monitor window.

Notice that there are four distinct parts of the movie. At the end of the movie, the image fades to black and remains black for about two seconds. You will trim the excess black footage.

7 Move the current-time indicator to 37:00.

8 In the Timeline window, position the cursor over the end of the Cardiac_cycle.avi video track.

The cursor changes to a red bracket with a double-sided arrow.

9 Drag the end of the clip to the current-time indicator at 37:00 to decrease its duration.

Adobe Encore DVD changes the out point of the clip.

10 Click in an empty area of the Timeline window to deselect the clip.

11 Save the file. Name it **Lesson_07.ncor.**

Creating and naming chapter points

You'll create a chapter point for each of the four sections in the movie.

1 Move the current-time indicator to the first frame in the timeline.

2 Select the chapter point marker at 00:00.

The chapter point marker is a polygon with the number 1 in it; it's red when it's selected. Every timeline has a chapter point marker at the 00:00 frame.

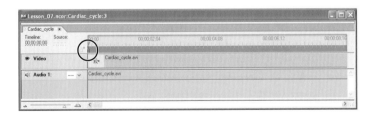

3 Choose Window > Properties to open the Properties palette.

Moving the current-time indicator

There are several ways to move the current-time indicator. Which method you use depends on your preference and how far you need to move the current-time indicator.

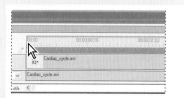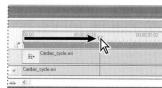

Drag the current-time indicator to the new location. This option is best if you're moving the current-time indicator a short distance. Otherwise, scrolling through the timeline can be time-consuming.

Click the timeline where you want the current-time indicator to be positioned. You can scroll rapidly through the timeline to the new position. When you click the timeline, the current-time indicator moves there.

Specify a numeric value in the Timeline field. Click the field and then type a new timecode value for the current-time indicator. When you press Enter, the current-time indicator moves to that location.

Drag left or right over the Timeline or Source timecode value. You can scrub through values, just as you can in Adobe Premiere or Adobe After Effects. The farther you drag, the more quickly the timecode changes.

4 In the Name field, type **Stage 1**.

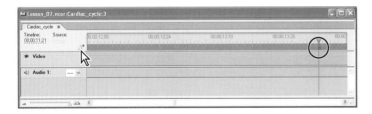

Naming the chapter points makes it easier to identify them when you create links later. You can name the chapter points to reflect the content of each chapter in the video.

5 Move the current-time indicator to 11:21.

There are several different ways to move the current-time indicator to different points on the timeline. See "Moving the current-time indicator" on page 160 to learn about them. The method you choose depends on your workflow and the length of the video clip you're using.

6 Click the Add Chapter button in the Timeline window.

A chapter point marker, labeled 2, appears at 11:21. You can also create a chapter point by right-clicking the handle of the current-time indicator and choosing Add Chapter Point.

Note: Video footage is divided into contiguous Groups of Pictures (GOPs), which are typically 13 frames long. When you're working with an MPEG-2 file, you can set a chapter point only at the first frame of a GOP, called a GOP header. If you attempt to insert a chapter point at a different frame, Adobe Encore DVD actually creates the chapter point at the previous GOP header. When working with an AVI file, as in this lesson, the same restrictions do not apply because the file has not yet been transcoded. Therefore, you can create a chapter point wherever you want it. When Adobe Encore DVD transcodes the AVI file, it automatically creates a GOP header at every chapter point you've set. To ensure both DVD compliance and best-quality transcoding, place chapter points in AVI videos at least 15 frames apart.

7 In the Properties palette, rename the chapter point **Stage 2**.

8 Create additional chapter points, named **Stage 3** and **Stage 4**, at 19:05 and 26:16, respectively.

9 Save the project.

Specifying an end action and a link for a timeline

You will link the Play Movie button to the video timeline, and then specify an end action for the timeline.

1 Select the Cardiac_cycle timeline in the Project window.

2 In the Properties palette, choose Cardiac_main > Play Stages from the End Action pop-up menu.

When the video finishes, the default behavior will be to return to the main menu, with the Play Stages button highlighted.

3 Open the Cardiac_main menu if it isn't already open. In the Menu Editor window, use the selection tool to select the Play Movie button.

4 In the Properties palette, choose Cardiac_cycle > Stage 1 from the Link pop-up menu.

When the Play Movie button is activated, the entire movie will play.

5 In the Project window, make sure the Cardiac_main menu is set for First Play.

Remember that the First Play item is denoted by an arrow icon. If the Cardiac_main menu is not set to play first, right-click it and choose Set as First Play.

6 Choose File > Preview. Press the Play Movie button to verify that the link and end action are working correctly.

When you press the Play Movie button, the entire movie should play, and then you should return to the main menu, with the Play Stages button highlighted.

7 Close the Project Preview window, and save the project.

Adding video to the background of a menu

Currently, the project has a still menu. Now you'll replace the still background layer with a moving background layer.

1 Make sure the Cardiac_main menu is open in the Menu Editor window.

2 Open the Layers palette.

The Layers palette lists the Background layer and the Background layer set. Click the eye icon (●) to hide and reveal the Background layer set and the Background layer.

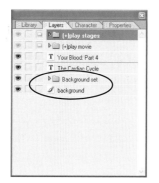

3 Select the Background layer set in the Layers palette, and then choose Edit > Clear to delete the layer set.

💡 *You can also press the Delete key on your keyboard to delete a layer or layer set. Make sure you've selected the appropriate layer or layer set, as Adobe Encore DVD does not prompt you to confirm the deletion. If you accidentally delete the wrong layer, choose Edit > Undo Clear Objects.*

4 Select the Project window to make it active, and then choose File > Import as Asset. Import the **Cardiac_background.avi** file.

5 Select the new AVI file in the Project window. Press the arrow next to the thumbnail preview in the Project window.

The video thumbnail plays, so that you can preview the video asset quickly. This clip is a short looping background. You will use it to replace the original background for the main menu.

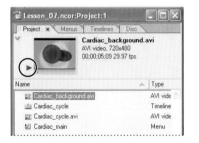

6 In the Project window, select the Cardiac_main menu.

7 In the Properties palette, drag the Video field pick whip (⊚) to the Cardiac_background.avi file in the Project window.

To use a pick whip, click the pick whip icon and then hold down the mouse button while you drag it to the item you want to pick. Release the mouse button when the item you want to select is highlighted. The item's name appears in the field.

The first frame of the Cardiac_background.avi file appears as the background.

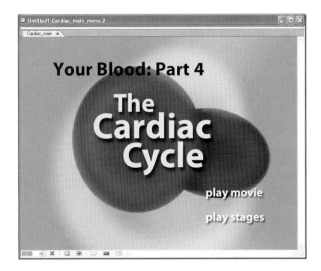

8 Save the project.

Previewing the motion menu background

By default, motion menus preview as still menus. To see a preview of the moving background, you must render it first. When you preview the motion menu, you can decide whether you need to make any adjustments, such as changing the number of times it loops.

1 Choose File > Render Motion Menus. Click Preview When Complete in the dialog box that contains the status bar.

When Adobe Encore DVD finishes rendering the motion menu, it opens in the Project Preview window. The background video plays behind the text and buttons on the menu. After the video plays, the screen turns black.

You'll change the number of times this video loops, so the video will play longer.

2 Close the Project Preview window.

3 In the Project window, select the Cardiac_main menu.

4 In the Properties palette, choose Forever from the Loop # pop-up menu.

5 Choose File > Preview.

This time, the video background plays once and then loops to play again.

💡 *When the video loops, a black screen may appear for a moment, or the video may pause. The looping point should be less obvious on the disc after you burn the final DVD project, but it may still be apparent. To avoid or minimize the pause, design the background video to appear from black at the start and fade to black at the end, or use a background video that is long enough that most viewers would make a selection before the loop point occurs.*

6 Close the Project Preview window, and save the project.

Transcoding an AVI file from the Project window

Transcoding is the process by which Adobe Encore DVD converts non-DVD-compliant video and audio asset files (such as AVI files) to the DVD-compliant files that will be burned to disc. (Files such as MPEG-2 files are already DVD-compliant and do not require transcoding.)You can transcode a file at any point during the project; if you have not already transcoded a non-DVD-compliant file, Adobe Encore DVD automatically transcodes it when you burn the disc. You can transcode assets directly from the Project window. Upon transcoding a file, Adobe Encore DVD updates the project link so that it points to the transcoded file. So, unless you delete the original file, you can also revert transcoded assets to their original version.

1 In the Project window, right-click Cardiac_background.avi and choose Transcode Settings > NTSC DV 4x3 High Quality 4Mb VBR 2 Pass.

Now that you have selected the transcoding setting, you can transcode the AVI file into an MPEG-2 file.

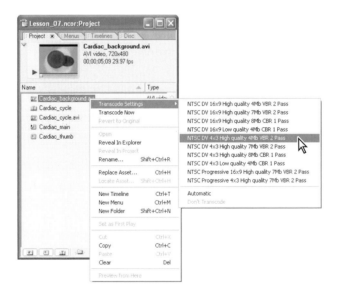

2 Right-click the Cardiac_background.avi file, and choose Transcode Now.

The Transcode Progress dialog box appears as Adobe Encore DVD transcodes the file. The Cardiac_background.avi file appears in the Project window even after it has been transcoded.

Note: To revert a transcoded asset to the original asset, right-click it in the Project window and choose Revert to Original.

3 If necessary, stretch the Project window so that you can see the Transcode Settings column.

The Project window shows that the file has been transcoded. Adobe Encore DVD uses the transcoded asset as you continue to author, preview, and build your DVD project.

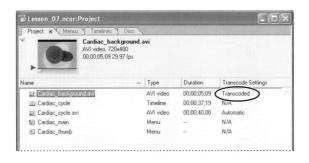

Creating video thumbnail buttons

In addition to naming a button, you can add a thumbnail of the video it links to. The thumbnail helps viewers identify each video more clearly, and adds interest to your menu. You can use still thumbnails, which display only a single frame of the video, or animated thumbnails, which play as much of the video as you specify.

Exploring a menu with thumbnail layers

Just as you can designate Adobe Photoshop layers as buttons and subpictures, you can also designate layers as thumbnails for use in buttons. The Library palette in Adobe Encore DVD contains several buttons that include thumbnail layers. Look at the layers in Photoshop to see how thumbnails are represented.

1 Open Adobe Photoshop. Choose File > Open, and then navigate to the Lesson 07 folder. Open the **Cardiac_thumb.psd** file.

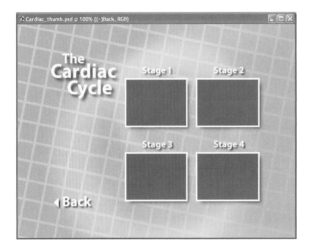

2 In the Photoshop Layers palette, expand the (+) Stage 1 button layer set.

To expand a layer set, click the arrow next to its name.

3 Notice that there is a red rectangle in the layer with (%) in its name.

Adobe Encore DVD recognizes layers and layer sets whose names begin with (%). In this case, the thumbnail is red just to help you identify it; Adobe Encore DVD will ignore the red color.

4 Exit Photoshop without saving the file.

Creating thumbnails from frames in a timeline

In this project, you'll create thumbnail buttons that are linked to frames in the video.

1 In Adobe Encore DVD, choose File > Import as Menu, and then import the **Cardiac_thumb.psd** file you just viewed in Photoshop.

The rectangles that were red in Photoshop appear semitransparent gray in Adobe Encore DVD.

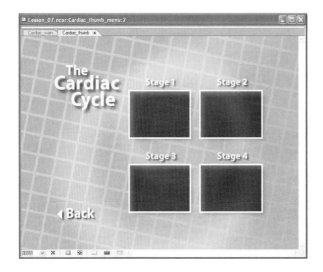

2 In the Project window, double-click the Cardiac_cycle timeline.

3 Move the current-time indicator to 00:00.

4 Drag the chapter point marker at 00:00 to the rectangle for the Stage 1 button in the Menu Editor window.

A thumbnail version of the first frame of the video appears in the button.

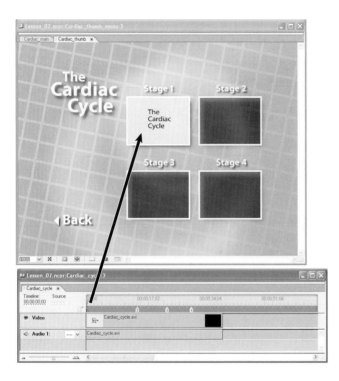

5 Drag the other three chapter point markers to their respective buttons.

Each button should display a frame with a number in it. However, the frame in the Stage 1 button shows the video title, and the frame in the Stage 4 button shows the number 3. First, you'll adjust the Stage 4 button to capture the appropriate frame.

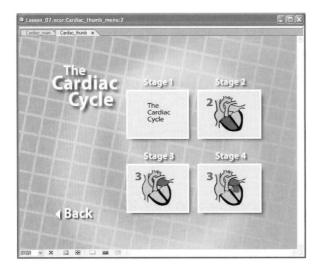

6 Zoom the timeline out to its maximum size.

Zooming lets you select single frames in the timeline with greater accuracy.

7 Scroll until the Stage 4 chapter point is visible in the timeline (26:16).

8 Move the Stage 4 chapter point marker to the right one frame at a time.

The image in the linked thumbnail button is updated as you move the marker.

9 When the Stage 4 button displays the frame that contains the number 4, release the marker.

10 Save the project.

Setting a poster frame

The first thumbnail button accurately displays the first frame of the video. When the viewer activates that button, you want the video to play from the first frame. However, because the first frame of the movie is different from the first frame of each section of the movie, the buttons don't appear consistent. To make the buttons consistent, set a different frame to appear in the thumbnail, without changing the frame that plays when the button is activated.

1 Move the current-time indicator to the point in the video where the first frame of the animated heart appears (03:03).

2 If necessary, scroll the timeline so that you can see the first chapter point. Leave the current-time indicator at 03:03.

3 Right-click the Stage 1 chapter point, and choose Set Poster Frame from the context menu.

The thumbnail button in the menu now shows the first frame of the heart animation. However, when the viewer activates this button, the video will begin playing at the first frame.

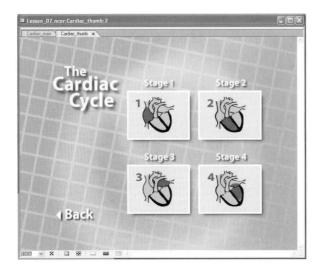

4 Save the project.

Setting behaviors

You've created the thumbnails. Now you'll set behaviors to ensure that viewers return to the thumbnail menu after they view a video using a thumbnail button.

1 In the Menu Editor window, select the Back button.

2 In the Properties palette, choose Cardiac_main > Play Movie from the Link pop-up menu.

When the viewer activates the Back button, the main menu will appear, with Play Movie highlighted.

3 In the Project window, click the Menus tab.

Only the menus in the project appear in the Menus tab.

4 Select the Cardiac_thumb menu.

The lower pane lists all the buttons contained in the selected menu. You can use this pane to organize buttons and to set some behaviors for multiple buttons more quickly.

5 Select all the buttons except the Back button. Make sure the Properties palette is open and displays the attributes for the selected buttons.

6 From the Override pop-up menu, choose Cardiac_thumb > Stage 1.

You've set the override behavior for all four buttons at once. Earlier, you set the default end action for the Cardiac_cycle timeline to return to the Cardiac_main menu, but the overrides ensure that the thumbnail menu will appear after the video is played from one of the thumbnail buttons.

7 In the Menu Editor window, click the Cardiac_main tab.

8 Select the Play Stages button.

9 In the Properties palette, link the Play Stages button to Cardiac_thumb > Stage 1.

10 Save the project.

Creating animated thumbnail buttons

Earlier you added moving video to the background for the main menu. Now you'll animate the thumbnail buttons in the second menu.

1 In the Project window, select the Cardiac_thumb menu.

2 In the Properties palette, select Animate Buttons.

3 Type **04:00** in the Duration field, and choose Forever from the Loop # pop-up menu.

Note: Make sure you enter the time in the Duration field and not the Loop Point field.

4 Choose File > Render Motion Menus.

Just as you needed to render motion menus in order to see the moving background for your menu, you need to render motion menus to preview animated thumbnail buttons. If you do not render the menus, you'll see still images in the preview.

5 In the Project window, right-click the Cardiac_thumb menu, and choose Preview From Here.

💡 *By choosing Preview From Here, you can begin previewing the project from the point you selected, without having to navigate through other menus.*

The menu opens, and the thumbnails display the first four seconds of video from their respective points on the timeline, and then loop. Again, there may be a slight delay when the video loops.

💡 *Use After Effects to create animated buttons and motion menu backgrounds. After Effects is designed for adding special effects to video, so you can use a wider variety of tools and features to achieve the effect you want. In Lesson 9, you'll use After Effects and Adobe Encore DVD together.*

Burning the DVD

Burn the project to disc using any of the methods described in previous lessons. The method used in Lesson 1 follows.

1 In the Project window, click the Disc tab.

2 Change the disc name to **Lesson_07**.

3 From the pop-up menu beneath the disc name, choose the data size of the disc you'll be burning.

4 Click Build Project.

5 In the Make DVD Disc dialog box, choose Current Project from the Create Using pop-up menu, and choose your DVD recorder from the Recorder pop-up menu.

6 Insert a blank disc into the recorder, and click Next.

7 Review the information in the Make DVD Disc Summary dialog box. When you are ready to proceed, click Build.

Review questions

1 How can you trim a video clip in Adobe Encore DVD?

2 What is a motion menu?

3 How does Adobe Encore DVD recognize thumbnail layers?

4 What must you do before previewing a motion menu?

5 How can you configure a button to play a video while the viewer decides which button to choose?

6 Why do you need to transcode an AVI file?

Review answers

1 Move the cursor over the end of the clip in the Timeline window, until the cursor becomes a bracket. Then drag the cursor to the new end point for the video.

2 A motion menu is a menu that contains a moving background, animated buttons, audio, or any combination of the three. Essentially, a motion menu is any menu that is not static.

3 Adobe Encore DVD recognizes layers whose names contain (%) as thumbnails.

4 To preview a motion menu, you must first render it. Choose File > Render Motion Menus. If you preview a motion menu before rendering it, Adobe Encore DVD displays it as a still menu in the Project Preview window.

5 Select the button, select Animate Buttons in the Properties palette, and then specify how long you want the video to play and how many times it should loop.

6 AVI files are not DVD-compliant, so you must transcode them in order to burn them to a disc. You can transcode an AVI file at any time during your project, or you can let Adobe Encore DVD automatically transcode the file when it burns the DVD.

Lesson 8

8 Working with Adobe Premiere Pro

Video is at the heart of most DVD projects. Use Adobe Encore DVD and Adobe Premiere Pro together to achieve the best-quality video, and to arrange it in the most accessible way. The Edit Original command in Adobe Encore DVD lets you return to Premiere quickly to make changes to the video when necessary.

Adobe Encore DVD works smoothly with Adobe Premiere Pro to help you achieve the best results for your video DVD projects. Use Premiere Pro to prepare the assets for your DVD project, and then import them into Adobe Encore DVD. If you need to make changes to the assets, you can use the Edit Original command to open and edit the Premiere Pro project. When you've finished, the files update automatically in Adobe Encore DVD. In this lesson, you will learn how to do the following:

- Add sequence markers in Premiere Pro.

- Export a Premiere Pro sequence as a DVD-legal MPEG-2 file.

- Export a Premiere Pro sequence as an AVI file for use in Adobe Encore DVD.

- Create thumbnail buttons from chapter points in Adobe Encore DVD.

- Embed project information in an AVI file so that you can edit the original later.

- Use the Edit Original command in Adobe Encore DVD.

Getting started

Before you assemble your DVD project, you can edit and polish your video assets in Adobe Premiere Pro. You'll prepare an MPEG-2 file and an AVI file in Premiere Pro. You'll add sequence markers to the MPEG-2 file for use as chapter point markers in Adobe Encore DVD. And you'll edit the original project in Premiere Pro after importing the AVI file into Adobe Encore DVD.

In this lesson, you'll work in Premiere Pro and Adobe Encore DVD to create a new DVD project, using graphic and video files included on the *Adobe Encore DVD Classroom in a Book* DVD. Make sure you know the location of the files you need for Lesson 8. For help, see "Copying the Classroom in a Book files" on page 2.

To complete this lesson, you'll also need to have Adobe Premiere Pro installed on your computer.

Viewing the finished Adobe Encore DVD project

To see what you'll be creating, take a look at the finished project:

1 Start Adobe Encore DVD.

2 Choose File > Open Project.

3 In the Open dialog box, navigate to the Lesson 08 folder. Double-click the **Lesson_08_end folder**, select **Lesson_08_end.ncor,** and then click Open.

4 Choose File > Preview.

The Project Preview window opens, displaying a menu with two buttons.

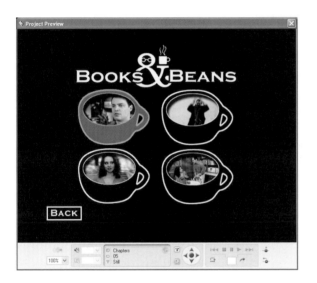

5 Click the Chapters button.

A second menu appears, containing four thumbnail buttons shaped like coffee cups as well as a Back button.

6 Click the thumbnail buttons in the menu to play the same video with different starting points.

7 Click the Back button to return to the first menu.

8 Click the Excerpt button.

A longer video plays, and then the main menu reappears.

9 Close the Project Preview window and the Lesson_08_end Project window.

Creating markers in Premiere Pro

First, you'll create sequence markers in a video in Premiere Pro where you want chapter markers to appear in Adobe Encore DVD.

1 Open Premiere Pro.

2 Click Open Project in the Welcome to Adobe Premiere Pro dialog box.

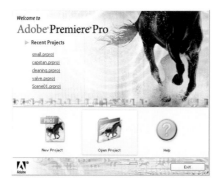

3 Navigate to the Lesson 08 folder. Select the **Trailer.prproj** file, and click Open.

Note: If you are prompted to locate the Trailer.avi file, navigate to the Premiere Source folder, and select the file.

The Premiere Pro project opens, with one AVI file in the Timeline window. If the Timeline window is not visible, double-click Sequence 01 in the Project window.

You'll preview the file in the Monitor window.

4 Click the Play button for the Sequence 01 tab in the Monitor window. The AVI file plays.

You'll add sequence markers to the timeline, and then export the sequence as an MPEG-2 file. Adobe Encore DVD will interpret the sequence markers as chapter point markers when you import the file.

5 Click the current time in the Timeline window. Change it to **03:21**, and then press Enter.

The current-time indicator moves to 03:21.

6 Choose Marker > Set Sequence Marker > Unnumbered.

Premiere Pro places a marker in the timeline at 03:21.

7 Change the current time to **12:20**.

8 Choose Marker > Set Sequence Marker > Unnumbered.

9 Repeat steps 7 and 8 to place sequence markers at **17:19** and **21:15**.

10 Save the project.

Exporting an MPEG-2 file from Premiere Pro

You'll use the Adobe Media Encoder to export the video file as an MPEG-2 file from Premiere Pro.

1 Choose File > Export > Adobe Media Encoder.

The Transcode Settings dialog box appears.

2 Choose MPEG2-DVD from the Format pop-up menu.

3 Choose NTSC DV High Quality 4Mb VBR 2 Pass from the Preset pop-up menu.

4 Click OK.

5 Name the file **Trailer_markers**, and click Save.

Premiere Pro renders the file, which may take a few minutes. The timeline is exported as an MPEG-2 file that can be imported into Adobe Encore DVD. Premiere Pro and Adobe Encore DVD use the same encoder.

6 When the file has rendered, save the project, and then exit Premiere Pro.

About MPEG-2 files

There are advantages and disadvantages to any file format. Before exporting an MPEG-2 file for use in Adobe Encore DVD, consider the advantages and disadvantages.

Advantages

• *Adobe Encore DVD converts AVI files to MPEG-2 when you burn a DVD. Because there is no need to convert MPEG-2 files, you can burn DVDs more quickly when you use them.*

• *An MPEG-2 file has a smaller file size than an AVI file exported from the same Premiere Pro project.*

• *Most video-editing applications cannot edit MPEG-2 files, so the files are more secure.*

• *You can choose the transcode settings you use with MPEG-2 files.*

Disadvantages

• *Fewer applications can play MPEG-2 files, so if you are distributing MPEG-2 files separately from the DVD, viewers may not be able to play them.*

• *When you export a timeline in MPEG-2 format, two files are actually created: an M2V file for the video, and a WAV file for the audio. The chances of missing a component are much greater than they are with an AVI file, which contains both audio and video.*

• *You can create chapter points only at the GOP (Group of Pictures) points in an MPEG-2 file, so you may not be able to link a button to the specific frame you choose.*

Importing an MPEG-2 file with markers

You exported a Premiere Pro project as an MPEG-2 file that contains sequence markers. Now you'll import that MPEG-2 file into Adobe Encore DVD, which will recognize the markers as chapter point markers.

1 Open Adobe Encore DVD.

2 Choose File > New Project. Click OK to accept NTSC as the television standard.

3 Choose File > Import as Asset.

4 Navigate to the Premiere Source folder inside the Lesson_08 folder, where you saved the MPEG-2 file from Premiere Pro. Select **Trailer_markers.m2v** and **Trailer_markers.wav**.

When you exported the timeline from Premiere Pro, it created two files: an MPEG-2 file for the video content, and a WAV file for the audio content.

5 In the Project window, select the Trailer_markers.m2v file.

6 Choose Timeline > New Timeline.

A new timeline opens with the Trailer_markers.m2v file on the video track. The Monitor window opens.

7 Click the Zoom-out icon in the bottom-left corner of the Timeline window so that you can see the entire video track.

The four markers you created in Premiere Pro appear in the timeline as numbered chapter point markers, even though the markers you created in Premiere Pro were unnumbered. Additionally, Adobe Encore DVD has added a chapter point at the first frame of the track. There is a chapter point at the first frame of every timeline in Adobe Encore DVD.

8 Drag the Trailer_markers.wav file from the Project window onto the Audio 1 track in the Timeline window.

9 Click the Play button in the Monitor window to view the timeline.

10 Save the project as **Lesson_08.ncor**.

Though Adobe Encore DVD is a Windows-only application, you can use it to burn DVDs that contain video files you've saved in Mac OS or in QuickTime format. Open the video file in Premiere Pro, and export it as an MPEG-2 file. Then import the MPEG-2 file into Adobe Encore DVD. To convert QuickTime files to MPEG-2 files, Premiere Pro requires that certain QuickTime files be installed.

Linking chapter points to thumbnail buttons

To give your viewers information about the video they'll see when they click a button, add a thumbnail image of the video to the button. When you create the thumbnail, Adobe Encore DVD automatically links it to its chapter point.

1 Click the Project window to make it active. Choose File > Import as Menu.

2 Navigate to the Lesson 08 folder. Select **Chapters.psd**, and click Open.

The menu opens in the Menu Editor window. It includes four buttons shaped as coffee cups, which you will link to chapter points in the timeline. When one of the buttons is activated, the video will play from the chapter point linked to that button.

3 Position the Trailer_markers timeline and the Menu Editor window so that they are both visible.

4 Drag chapter point 2 to the elliptical shape in the upper-left coffee cup.

A thumbnail image appears in the cup. Adobe Encore DVD automatically creates a link between the button and the chapter point in the timeline.

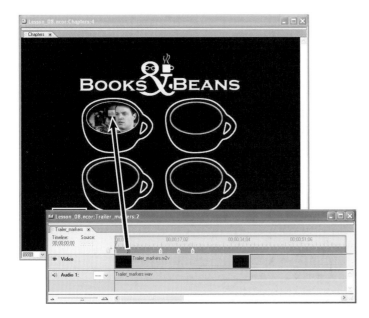

5 Drag chapter point 3 to the upper-right cup, chapter point 4 to the lower-right cup, and chapter point 5 to the lower-left cup.

When you click a button, the video will play from the point in the timeline associated with the marker to the end of the timeline. You want the Chapters menu to reappear after the timeline plays, so you will set an end action for the timeline.

6 Make sure the Trailer_markers timeline is active. If necessary, click the Trailer_markers timeline in the Project window.

Note: Make sure you click the Trailer_markers timeline and not the Trailer_markers.m2v file.

7 If the Properties window is not open, choose Window > Properties.

The Properties window displays the attributes for the Trailer_markers timeline.

8 Choose Chapters > 1 from the End Action pop-up menu.

When the timeline finishes, the menu will reappear.

9 Save the project.

Previewing the project

You've set the links for the Chapters menu. Before you continue with the project, preview this section to ensure that it behaves as you expect.

1 In the Project window, right-click the Chapters menu, and choose Preview From Here.

The Project Preview window opens, displaying the Chapters menu. One of the cups is highlighted.

2 Move the cursor over the other cups, and then click one of the cups.

Creating thumbnails with interesting shapes

Adobe Encore DVD creates thumbnails as rectangles, to match the frame of the video. To display a thumbnail with a more interesting shape, such as the ovals you're using in this project, first make a rectangle and then mask it.

In Photoshop, when you create a video thumbnail button with a nonrectangular shape, the actual thumbnail layer should be rectangular. If the layer is not rectangular, Adobe Encore DVD calculates the smallest rectangle in which the image could fit. The video remains rectangular regardless of the shape of the image layer.

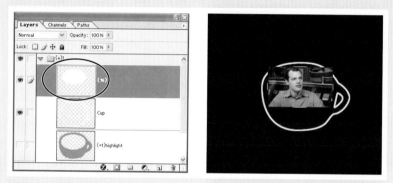

This button was created with an elliptical layer.

You can, however, use vector masks or layer masks on the thumbnail layer to create a nonrectangular shape. The size of the image determines the size of the video displayed in the menu.

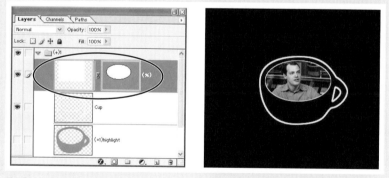

This button was created with a rectangular layer and an elliptical vector mask.

As you move the cursor over a cup, it is highlighted. When you click a cup, the video plays from the chapter point associated with the button, and when the video is finished, the menu reappears.

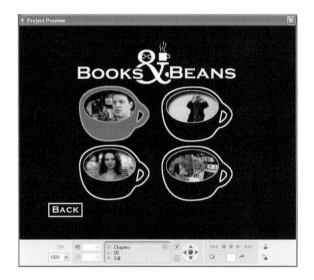

3 Close the Project Preview window.

Exporting an AVI file from Premiere Pro

Earlier, you exported an MPEG-2 file from Premiere Pro. Now you'll export the excerpt video as an AVI file.

1 Open Premiere Pro.

2 Click Open Project in the Welcome to Adobe Premiere Pro dialog box.

3 Navigate to the Lesson 08 folder. Select **Scene01.prproj**, and click Open.

Note: If you are prompted to locate the Clip01.avi file, navigate to the Premiere Source folder and select the file.

If the Timeline window is not visible, double-click Sequence 01 in the Project window.

4 Click the Play button for the Sequence 01 tab in the Monitor window.

There are multiple clips in the timeline for this project. It is ready to export.

5 Click the Timeline window to ensure that the timeline is active, and choose File > Export > Movie.

6 In the Export Movie dialog box, name the file **Scene01**.

7 Click Settings.

8 In the Export Movie Settings dialog box, choose Microsoft DV AVI from the File Type pop-up menu and Work Area Bar from the Range pop-up menu.

9 Select Export Video and Export Audio.

10 Choose Project from the Embedding Options pop-up menu, and then click OK.

When Premiere Pro renders the AVI file, information about the Premiere Pro project will be included in the file. Because this information is included, you'll be able to open the Premiere Pro project using the Edit Original command in Adobe Encore DVD or Adobe After Effects.

11 Click Save.

If you are prompted to save the Premiere Pro project first, click Yes.

12 When Premiere Pro has finished rendering the file, close the project and exit from Premiere Pro.

About AVI files

The advantages and disadvantages of using AVI files are the inverse of those for MPEG-2 files.

Advantages

• *More applications play AVI files, so you can distribute them more widely, separate from the DVD you burn.*

• *You can edit AVI files in most video-editing applications.*

• *A single file contains both the audio and video components.*

• *You can place chapter points wherever you want them.*

Disadvantages

• *Because Adobe Encore DVD converts AVI files to MPEG-2 files when burning to disc, projects that use AVI files can take longer to burn.*

• *AVI files usually have larger file sizes than comparable MPEG-2 files.*

• *You can't choose the transcode settings for an AVI file.*

Using the Edit Original command

When you need to make a change in a file you exported from Premiere Pro, use the Edit Original command in Adobe Encore DVD. In this project, you will remove part of the video from the middle of the timeline.

1 Open the Adobe Encore DVD project.

2 Choose File > Import as Asset, and select the **Scene01.avi** file. Click Open.

3 Select the Scene01.avi file in the Project window, and click the Create a New Timeline button ( ) at the bottom of the Project window.

Adobe Encore DVD creates a timeline for the AVI file, and opens the Monitor window.

4 Click the Play button in the Monitor window to view the AVI file.

You will remove the portion of the clip that shows the tombstones. You could use Adobe Encore DVD to trim the in point or the out point of a video, but you need to use Premiere Pro to remove a section from the middle of the clip.

5 In the Project window, select the Scene01.avi video file.

Note: Make sure you select the video file, and not the timeline.

6 Choose Edit > Edit Original.

Because you embedded project information when you rendered the AVI file in Premiere Pro, the project from which you exported the file opens. If Premiere Pro is not currently running, it will start automatically.

Using the ripple edit tool in Premiere Pro

The ripple edit tool lets you trim a clip within a timeline, and then adjusts the clips that follow. You will use the ripple edit tool to remove the tombstone scene from the video.

1 In Premiere Pro, click the timeline to ensure that it is active.

2 In the Timeline window, move the current-time indicator to 20:19 (right before the scene of the tombstones).

This is where you want this clip to end, editing out the tombstones.

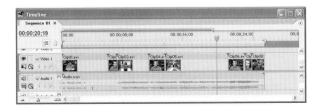

3 Select the ripple edit tool (⊷) in the toolbox.

4 Move the cursor to the right edge (the end) of Clip05 in the timeline. When the cursor changes to a red bracket with a double arrow (⬌), drag it to the current-time indicator.

A ripple edit trims a clip and shifts subsequent clips in the track by the amount you trim. However, it has no effect on the audio track. You'll need to trim the audio track separately.

5 Select the selection tool in the toolbox.

6 Place the cursor over the right edge of the audio track, and drag it until the right edge of the audio track is even with the right edge of the video track.

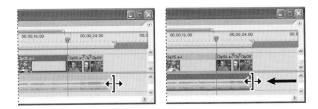

7 Save the project.

Updating an AVI file in Adobe Encore DVD

You'll export the movie again, and then return to Adobe Encore DVD. The AVI file will be automatically updated.

1 Make sure the timeline is active and choose File > Export > Movie.

2 In the Export Movie dialog box, verify that the name of the file is Scene01.avi, and that you're saving it to the same folder as the original.

3 Click Save.

4 Click Yes in the dialog box that warns you that you'll be replacing a file with the same name.

5 When Premiere Pro has finished rendering the file, close the project.

6 Return to Adobe Encore DVD.

The AVI file should update automatically.

7 Play the timeline in the Monitor window.

The AVI file has been updated in Adobe Encore DVD. When you play the timeline in the Monitor window, the video plays as you edited it in Premiere Pro.

Creating links and behaviors

With the assets and menus in place, all that remains is to create the links and set the behaviors for the menu buttons and timelines.

1 Click the Project window to make it active. Then choose File > Import as Menu, and select **Main.psd**. Click Open.

A new menu with two buttons appears in the Menu Editor window.

2 With the selection tool, select the Excerpt button.

3 In the Properties palette, choose Scene01 > Chapter 1 from the Link pop-up menu.

When the Excerpt button is activated, the Scene01 timeline will play.

4 Select the Chapters button.

5 In the Properties palette, choose Chapters > 1 from the Link pop-up menu.

When the Chapters button is activated, the Chapters menu will appear, with the first button highlighted.

6 Click the Scene01 timeline in the Project window to make it active.

7 Choose Main > Chapters from the End Action pop-up menu in the Properties palette.

When the Scene01 timeline finishes playing, the Main menu will display, with the Chapters button highlighted.

8 Choose Main > Chapters from the Menu Remote pop-up menu.

If the viewer presses the Menu button during the Scene01 timeline, the Main menu will appear.

9 Click the Chapters tab in the Menu Editor window to make that menu active.

Note: If there is no Chapters tab, double-click the Chapters menu in the Project window to open it in the Menu Editor window.

10 In the Menu Editor window, use the selection tool to select the Back button.

11 In the Properties palette, choose Main > Chapters from the Link pop-up menu.

12 Save the project.

Previewing the project

You've almost completed the entire DVD project. Now specify the file that will play first, and then preview the navigation in the project.

1 In the Project window, right-click the Main menu, and choose Set as First Play.

When the DVD is inserted, the Main menu will appear on the television or monitor.

2 Choose File > Preview.

The Project Preview window opens, displaying the Main menu.

3 Click the buttons in the menu, or use the remote control buttons at the bottom of the Project Preview window, to navigate the project.

4 When you have checked all of the links and behaviors, close the Project Preview window.

5 Save the project.

Burning the disc

Burn the project to a DVD.

1 In the Project window, click the Disc tab.

2 Change the disc name to **Lesson_08**.

3 From the pop-up menu beneath the disc name, choose the data size of the disc you'll be burning.

4 Click Project Settings. In the Project Settings dialog box, you can specify whether the disc is the first or second side of a dual-sided disc, assign a region code, and enable copy protection. Each of these options is activated only if you burn the project to a digital linear tape (DLT) for mass replication. Click OK to close the dialog box.

Note: Each region code corresponds to a particular area of the world; a DVD player plays a DVD only if it recognizes the region code. By default, all regions are enabled, so if you write directly to a DVD, any player should be able to play your disc.

5 Click Build Project.

6 In the Make DVD Disc dialog box, choose Current Project from the Create Using pop-up menu, and choose your DVD recorder from the Recorder pop-up menu.

7 Insert a blank disc into the recorder, and click Next.

8 Review the information in the Make DVD Disc Summary dialog box. When you are ready to proceed, click Build.

Review questions

1 How can you include chapter point markers in an MPEG-2 file you export from Premiere Pro?

2 What files does Premiere Pro create when you export an MPEG-2 file?

3 How can you ensure that you'll be able to edit a Premiere Pro project from within Adobe Encore DVD or After Effects after you've exported the project as an AVI file?

4 When would you use the ripple edit tool in Premiere Pro?

5 What are the advantages of MPEG-2 files?

6 What are the advantages of AVI files?

Review answers

1 Add unnumbered sequence markers to the timeline in Premiere Pro. When it imports the MPEG-2 file, Adobe Encore DVD recognizes the sequence markers as chapter point markers, and numbers them. It also adds a chapter point to the beginning of the timeline.

2 When you export an MPEG-2 file from Premiere Pro, it creates an .m2v file for the video content and a .wav file for the audio content.

3 To ensure that you can edit the original project from Adobe Encore DVD or After Effects after you've exported it as an AVI file, choose Project from the Embedding Options pop-up menu in the Export Movie Settings dialog box.

4 Use the ripple edit tool in Premiere Pro to trim a clip within a timeline. The clips that follow move forward or backward to accommodate the change.

5 MPEG-2 files have a smaller file size than AVI files. When you use MPEG-2 files, you can burn the DVD more quickly, because Adobe Encore DVD does not need to convert the files. The files are more secure, because they cannot be edited as easily in video-editing applications. Additionally, you can choose the transcode settings that are used.

6 You can play AVI files in a wider variety of applications than MPEG-2 files, and you can edit them in applications such as Premiere Pro. When you save an AVI file, the entire project is written to a single file. Additionally, you can place chapter points wherever you want them in AVI files.

Lesson 9

9 Working with Adobe After Effects

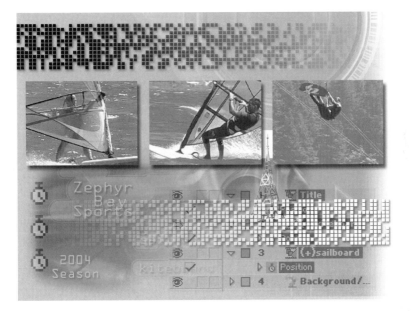

Bring the power of Adobe After Effects into your DVD project. Add special effects in After Effects, import the file into Adobe Encore DVD, and then return to After Effects at any time to make additional changes.

Pair Adobe Encore DVD with Adobe After Effects to leverage the features of both applications. You can import AVI files that you create in After Effects into Adobe Encore DVD, and return to After Effects to edit them at any time. In this lesson you will learn how to do the following:

• Import an After Effects file as an asset.

• Return to After Effects to edit the original file.

• Embed a project link in the rendered movie.

• Loop a motion menu in Adobe Encore DVD.

• Remove unneeded elements from an imported Photoshop menu.

Getting started

In this lesson, you'll use an After Effects movie as a background for a menu in Adobe Encore DVD, and pair it with a Photoshop menu to provide subpictures.

You'll use graphic and video files included on the *Adobe Encore DVD Classroom in a Book* DVD. Make sure you know the location of the files you need for Lesson 9. For help, see "Copying the Classroom in a Book files" on page 2.

To complete this project, you must also have Adobe After Effects 5.5 or later installed on your computer.

Viewing the finished Adobe Encore DVD project

To see what you'll be creating, take a look at the finished project:

1 Start Adobe Encore DVD.

2 Choose File > Open Project.

3 In the Open dialog box, navigate to the Lesson 09 folder. Double-click the **Lesson_09_end** folder, select **Lesson_09_end.ncor**, and then click Open.

4 Choose File > Preview.

The Project Preview window opens, and a looping menu appears.

5 Close the Project Preview window, and the Lesson_09_end Project window.

Importing a Photoshop menu

First, import the Photoshop menu into your project.

1 Choose File > New Project. Click OK to accept NTSC as the television standard.

2 Choose File > Import as Menu. Navigate to the Lesson 09 folder, and import the **Zephyr.psd file.**

The menu appears in Adobe Encore DVD.

3 Click on the menu in the Menu Editor window, and then open the Layers palette.

The menu includes a layer set for the title text; a background layer; and two additional layer sets, which Adobe Encore DVD recognizes as buttons.

4 Click the Show Selected Subpicture Highlight button at the bottom of the Menu Editor window to see the subpictures for the buttons.

The subpictures were defined in Photoshop. Adobe Encore DVD recognizes the layers as subpictures because their names begin with (=1).

5 Make the Character palette active by clicking the Character tab. Then choose OCR A Std for the font, Medium for the font style, and 36 for the type size. Click the Align Center option.

6 With the text tool, click an insertion point in the Menu Editor window, and type **2004**. Press Enter, and type **Season**.

7 With the selection tool, move the text block you just created to the bottom-left area of the menu.

8 With the text block still selected, choose Object > Drop Shadow. Accept the defaults in the Drop Shadow dialog box, and click OK.

9 Save the project as **Lesson_09.ncor.**

Modifying a Photoshop file in After Effects

Now you'll import the same Photoshop file into After Effects, and save it with a 10-second duration.

1 Open After Effects.

2 After Effects opens with a new, untitled project.

3 Choose File > Save As, and save the project as **Lesson_09.aep** in the same folder as the Lesson_09.ncor file.

4 Choose Composition > New Composition.

The Composition Settings dialog box opens.

5 Set the duration to 00:00:04:00 (4 seconds). Leave the other settings as they are, and click OK.

Comp 1 appears in the Project window. You will not use this composition, but when you import the Photoshop file into After Effects, the duration of the new composition and each of its layers will be eight seconds.

6 Select Comp 1 in the Project window and choose Edit > Clear.

The Project window is now empty.

7 Choose File > Import > File.

8 Select the **Zephyr.psd** file, and choose Composition from the Import As pop-up menu. Then click Open.

The Project window contains a folder and a comp, both named Zephyr.psd (After Effects 5.5) or Zephyr Comp 1 (After Effects 6.0). The folder contains the individual layers. The composition is made up of the assembled layers.

Note: If there is only one file in the Project window, you didn't import the layered Photoshop file as a composition (step 7). Delete the file and re-import it as a composition.

9 In the Project window, double-click the composition icon (not the folder) for Zephyr.psd or Zephyr Comp 1.

The Timeline and Composition window open. Each Photoshop layer or layer set is on a separate line in the timeline.

10 Choose Composition > Composition Settings.

11 Make sure the Preset is NTSC DV 720 x 480 (After Effects 5.5) or NTSC 720 x 480 (After Effects 6.0), and the duration is 00:00:04:00 (4 seconds). Then click OK.

12 Save the After Effects project.

Animating a menu file in After Effects

You imported a static Photoshop menu file. Now you'll animate the file so that the buttons and title move during the four seconds that the menu plays.

1 In the Timeline window, move the current-time indicator to 01:00 (1 second).

2 Select the first three layers in the timeline. (Hold down the Ctrl key to select multiple layers.)

3 Press the P key on your keyboard to display the Position property for each of the selected layers.

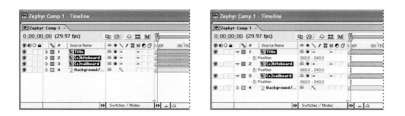

4 Click the stopwatches next to each of the Position properties to create a keyframe for the position of each layer.

5 Return the current-time indicator to 00:00.

6 Select the Title layer, and change its position to 930, 240.

You can change the position manually by selecting and dragging the title in the Comp window. Or you can click the numbers in the timeline and type new values.

7 Move the Kiteboard layer set to 710,240. Also move the Sailboard layer set to 710, 240.

8 Choose Composition > Preview > RAM Preview.

The title and buttons enter the screen from the right and then stop in their final positions.

9 Save the project.

Adding more animation

You have animated the layers so that they are off the screen at 0 seconds and enter from the right. Now you will add keyframes to move them off the screen again.

1 In the Timeline window, move the current-time indicator to 03:00 (3 seconds).

2 Press the Ctrl key as you click the word Position underneath the layer name for the top three layers.

3 Choose Animation > Add Keyframe.

A new keyframe is added to each layer; it has the same value as the keyframes in the 01:00 frame. You want the layers to stay in the same position from 01:00 to 03:00.

4 Click an empty area on the timeline to deselect the keyframes at 03:00. Then press the Shift key as you select the three position keyframes at the 01:00 frame. Choose Animation > Toggle Hold Keyframe.

You've ensured that the three layers will not change position until the next keyframe.

5 Click an empty area on the timeline to deselect the keyframes. Then move the current-time indicator to the last frame of the composition (03:29).

6 Move the Title layer's position to the left (-40, 240).

7 Move the Kiteboard layer set's position to -280, 240. Then, move the Sailboard layer set's position to -280, 240.

8 Choose Composition > Preview > RAM Preview.

The layers move onto the screen from the right, pause for two seconds, and then continue to move to the left until they are off the screen.

9 Save the project.

Adjusting keyframes to add interest

To make the animation a little more interesting, you will change the keyframes so that the title and buttons move at different times. Times are suggested in these instructions, but the exact times of the keyframes isn't critical. You can experiment with different times, using the RAM Preview command to view the results.

1 For the Title layer, drag the second keyframe (currently at 1 second) to 8 frames (00:08).

2 For the Kiteboard layer set, move the first keyframe (currently at 0 seconds) to 9 frames (00:09), and the second keyframe (currently at 1 second) to 18 frames (00:18).

3 For the Sailboard layer set, move the first keyframe (currently at 0 seconds) to 19 frames (00:19), and leave the second keyframe at 1 second (01:00).

4 Move the last two keyframes for each layer to create more interesting exits and entries.

Note: Make sure you don't change the order of the keyframes in a layer.

5 Choose Composition > Preview > RAM Preview.

The title and buttons move into the screen from the right at intervals, and exit the screen according to the keyframes you've created.

6 Save the After Effects project.

Rendering a movie in After Effects

You're ready to create the movie in After Effects.

1 Choose Composition > Make Movie.

If you are prompted to name the movie file, name it **Zephyr_background.avi**, and specify a folder for it. The Render Queue dialog box opens. Your project appears in the queue.

2 Click the value next to Render Settings for your project.

3 Choose Best from the Quality pop-up menu and Full from the Resolution pop-up menu. Then click OK.

4 Click the value next to Output Module in the Render Queue dialog box.

5 In the Output Module Settings dialog box, choose Project Link from the Embed pop-up menu.

Embedding a project link ensures that you can return to the After Effects file to edit it from Adobe Encore DVD, even though you'll be placing a rendered movie file—not the After Effects file itself—into your Adobe Encore DVD project.

6 Click Format Options in the Video Output section of the Output Module Settings dialog box.

7 Choose No Compression from the Compressor pop-up menu, and click OK. Click OK to close the Output Module Settings dialog box.

8 Click the name next to Output To in the Render Queue dialog box. If you haven't already named the file, name it **Zephyr_background.avi**, and specify a folder for it.

9 Click Render. If you are prompted to save the After Effects project, click OK.

After Effects renders the movie. Depending on your system, this may take a few minutes.

10 Leave the Render Queue open, and don't change the settings.

11 Save the After Effects project and close it.

Note: It is important to close the After Effects project.

Importing an After Effects movie into Adobe Encore DVD

You'll import the movie into Adobe Encore DVD as an asset. Though you'll use the movie in the menu, it is only a component of the menu. The Photoshop file you imported will provide the framework for the menu, so the subpictures will be intact.

1 In Adobe Encore DVD, click the Project window to make it active, and then choose File > Import as Asset.

2 Select the AVI file you just rendered in After Effects (**Zephyr_background.avi**), and click Open.

3 In the Project window, double-click the Zephyr menu to open the Menu Editor window, and then click the Layers tab or choose Window > Layers to open the Layers palette.

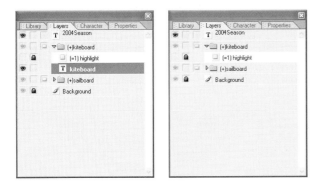

4 In the Layers palette, select the Title layer set and choose Edit > Clear.

The title disappears from the menu in the Menu Editor window.

5 Click the arrow next to the Kiteboard layer set to expand it. Then delete the text layer in it (named "Kiteboard").

The "kiteboard" text disappears from the Menu Editor window, but the Kiteboard layer set and the subpicture layer remain in the Layers palette.

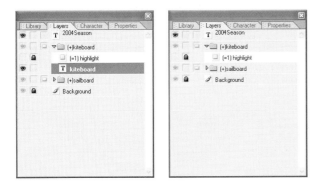

6 Delete the text layer from the Sailboard layer set in the same way.

The layer sets themselves, and the subpictures within them, should remain in the Layers palette.

7 Click the Show Selected Subpicture Highlight button at the bottom of the Menu Editor window to see the subpictures.

8 Press the Alt key while you drag the Zephyr_background.avi file from the Project window into the Menu Editor window.

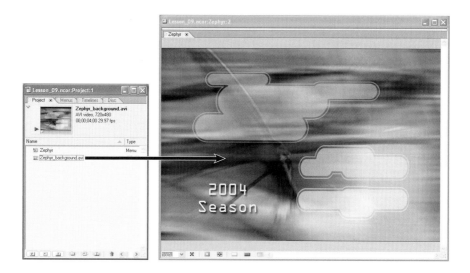

There is no apparent change in the Menu Editor window, because the text is off-screen at 0 seconds. However, the background has been replaced by the video asset you created in After Effects. The beginning frame of the movie should match the menu background perfectly.

Note: If a button appears, delete it and the new timeline it created in the Project window, and then be sure to press the Alt key while you drag the file into the Menu Editor window.

9 Select the Zephyr menu in the Project window, and open the Properties palette.

The Zephyr_background.avi file should be listed in the Video field in the Properties palette. If it isn't, press the Alt key as you drag the Zephyr_background.avi file into the Menu Editor window again.

10 Choose File > Render Motion Menus.

To display a menu in motion, Adobe Encore DVD must first render it. If you do not render the motion menu, Adobe Encore DVD will display it as a still menu.

11 Choose File > Preview.

The video plays once, and then a black screen appears.

12 Close the Project Preview window, and save the Adobe Encore DVD project.

Activating a motion menu

You animated the menu in After Effects. Now you will specify how the motion menu should behave in Adobe Encore DVD.

1 Select the Zephyr menu in the Project window.

2 In the Properties palette, leave the Duration at 4 seconds (04:00), and choose Forever from the Loop # pop-up menu.

The video will play until it reaches the end, and then loop until you make a selection.

3 Choose File > Render Motion Menus.

If File > Render Motion Menus is dimmed, go to step 4.

4 Choose File > Preview.

5 Close the Project Preview window, and save the project.

Editing a file in After Effects

Next, you will make the loop more interesting. You can easily edit the original file in After Effects, and update the file in Adobe Encore DVD, without disturbing the subpictures.

1 In Adobe Encore DVD, select the Zephyr_background.avi file in the Project window.

2 Choose Edit > Edit Original.

The After Effects project you used to create the AVI file opens in After Effects.

Note: If you are asked whether you want to open the original project version, click Yes. An untitled version of the After Effects file opens.

3 In the Timeline window, select the Background/Zephyr.psd layer.

4 Choose Edit > Duplicate.

A new duplicate layer of the background appears directly above the background layer.

5 With the new layer selected, choose Layer > Transfer Mode > Add (After Effects 5.5) or Layer > Blending Mode > Add (After Effects 6.0).

6 With the new layer still selected, press the T key on your keyboard to display the Opacity property for the layer.

7 Set the Opacity to 40%.

8 Drag the current-time indicator in the Timeline window to 2 seconds (02:00).

9 Click the stopwatch icon next to the Opacity value to create a keyframe.

10 Drag the current-time indicator to the left about 10 frames ((01:20).

11 Set the Opacity to 0%.

A new keyframe is automatically created.

12 Move the current-time indicator to about 02:10. Set the Opacity to 0%.

The keyframes you just created will make the new layer appear and then disappear, creating a glowing pulse in the animation.

13 Choose Composition > Preview > RAM Preview.

14 Save the After Effects project.

Rendering the movie

You'll render the movie again before returning to Adobe Encore DVD. If the Render Queue dialog box is open, and displays an output module with the same settings as the movie you originally rendered, just click Render and click OK to overwrite the existing file; then save and close the project. If the Render Queue dialog box is not open, or does not display the original settings, follow these steps to render the movie:

1 Click the Timeline window to make it active, and then choose Composition > Make Movie.

If you are prompted to name the movie file, name it **Zephyr_background.avi**, and specify a folder for it. The Render Queue window opens.

2 Click the value next to Render Settings.

3 Use the same settings as before: Best for Quality, and Full for Resolution. Then click OK.

4 Double-click Output Module, and then click Format Options in the Video Output section.

5 Choose No Compression from the Compressor pop-up menu, and click OK.

6 Choose Project Link and Copy from the Embed pop-up menu in the Output Module dialog box, and then click OK.

7 Click the filename next to Output To, and name the file **Zephyr_background.avi** if you haven't already named it.

8 A warning dialog box asks if you want to replace Zephyr_background.avi. Click Yes to overwrite the original.

9 Click Render.

If you're prompted to save the project, click OK.

10 When the file has finished rendering, save and close the project.

Returning to Adobe Encore DVD

The file you edited in After Effects will be updated in Adobe Encore DVD. You'll render the motion menu to see the full effect. Because the file has the same name, you'll re-link it to the menu before rendering motion menus.

1 Return to Adobe Encore DVD. In the Project window, select the Zephyr menu.

2 In the Properties palette, click the Video field, and then press Delete.

The Menu Editor window turns black, and the Video field contains the word "nothing."

3 Drag the Video pick whip from the Properties palette to the Zephyr_background.avi file in the Project window.

4 Choose File > Render Motion Menus.

Though you updated the After Effects file, Adobe Encore DVD didn't recognize the changes. Therefore, the Render Motion Menus command was dimmed. To render motion menus again, so that the file appears correctly in the preview, you deleted the Video link and re-created it.

5 Choose File > Preview.

6 Move the mouse over the buttons to see the subpictures appear.

7 Close the Project Preview window.

8 Save the project.

Creating links to assets

Now you'll link the buttons in the menu to timelines. First, import the videos and create the timelines.

1 Choose File > Import as Asset, and import the **Kite.avi** and **Sail.avi** files.

2 Select the AVI files in the Project window, and choose Timeline > New Timeline.

3 Click the Menus tab in the Project window, and select the Zephyr menu.

4 Select the Kiteboard button in the lower pane of the Menus tab. In the Properties palette, choose Kite > Chapter 1 from the Link pop-up menu.

5 Link the Sailboard button to Sail > Chapter 1.

6 Click the Timelines tab in the Project window.

7 Select the Kite and Sail timelines. In the Properties window, choose Zephyr > Default from the End Action pop-up menu.

8 Save the project.

9 Choose File > Render Motion Menus.

If File > Render Motion Menus is dimmed, go to step 4.

10 Choose File > Preview.

11 In the Project Preview window, test the links and end actions. When you're finished, close the Project Preview window.

Burning the DVD

Burn the DVD using the Build DVD command.

1 Choose File > Build DVD > Make DVD Disc.

2 Choose Current Project from the Create Using pop-up menu, and specify your DVD recorder.

3 Insert a blank disc, and click Next.

Review questions

1 How can you edit an After Effects file from Adobe Encore DVD?

2 What is a motion menu?

3 What setting must you choose in After Effects to be able to edit the original in Adobe Encore DVD?

4 If you're using a motion menu from After Effects, how can you include subpictures?

Review answers

1 Select the AVI file in the Project window in Adobe Encore DVD, and then choose Edit > Edit Original.

2 A motion menu is, quite simply, a menu that moves. You can use a video file as the background or for the buttons in your menu, or add an audio file to play while a menu is displayed.

3 To be able to return to your After Effects project from Adobe Encore DVD, you must choose Project Link from the Embed pop-up menu in the Output Module Settings dialog box before you render the movie. To open this dialog box, double-click Output Module in the Render Queue.

4 To include subpictures with an After Effects file, create a Photoshop file that includes subpictures to layer with your video file.

Lesson 10

10 Creating a Slideshow from Still Images

DVDs can showcase still images as well as video. Using Adobe Encore DVD, you can create a menu for each image to allow the viewer to navigate through the slideshow, or create a timeline from the images for a slideshow that advances automatically.

In addition to delivering high-quality digital video, a DVD can be an efficient way to present still images. For example, you can use Adobe Encore DVD to create looping slideshows for display in trade show kiosks, or to present an artist or photographer's portfolio. You can even create slideshows from existing presentations. In this lesson you will learn how to do the following:

• Create a slideshow from a set of menus.

• Copy buttons from one menu to another.

• Add an audio file to a menu.

• Create a timeline from a set of still images.

• Trim video clips to match an audio file.

• Organize assets in folders.

Getting started

In this lesson, you'll create slideshows, using graphic and video files included on the *Adobe Encore DVD Classroom in a Book* DVD. Make sure you know the location of the files you need for Lesson 10. For help, see "Copying the Classroom in a Book files" on page 2.

Viewing the finished Adobe Encore DVD project

To see what you'll be creating, take a look at the finished project.

1 Start Adobe Encore DVD.

2 Choose File > Open Project.

3 In the Open dialog box, navigate to the Lesson 10 folder. Select **Lesson_10_end.ncor,** and click Open.

4 Choose File > Preview.

The Project Preview window opens, and a menu appears. The menu has two buttons.

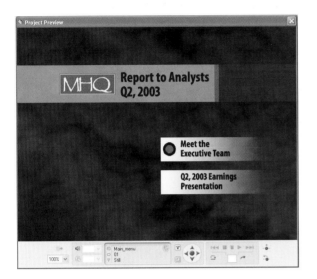

5 Click the Meet the Executive Team button. Click the Next button in the first two menus to progress through the slideshow. Click the Menu button in the last slideshow menu to return to the main menu.

6 Click the Q2 2003 Earnings Presentation button.

A slideshow plays, with the slides changing in time with audio cues.

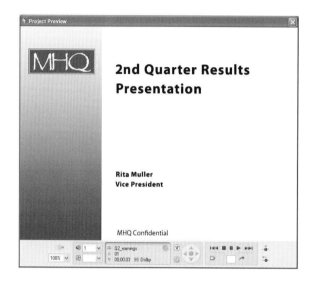

7 Close the Project Preview window and the Lesson_10_end Project window.

Assembling components for a slideshow

The first slideshow you'll create uses a method that provides a good way to display still images. Each image is on a separate menu, with navigational buttons to let the viewer move to the next image, the previous image, or the main menu. You'll import the menus and buttons into Adobe Encore DVD.

1 In Adobe Encore DVD, choose File > New Project. Click OK to accept NTSC as the television standard.

2 Choose File > Import as Menu. Navigate to the Lesson 10 folder. Select the **Main.psd**, **CFO.psd**, **Marketing.psd**, and **President.psd** files.

You have imported the main menu and three slideshow menus. The slideshow menus are single layer images—you will add buttons to them in Adobe Encore DVD. The main menu is a layered Adobe Photoshop menu, with buttons that were created in Photoshop.

This method is a good way to display a portfolio of still images. You can also adapt it to create a multiple-choice quiz.

3 In the Project window, right-click the Main.psd file and choose Set as First Play.

When the DVD is inserted into the player, the main menu will appear.

4 Close the Main.psd file in the Menu Editor window by clicking the "x" in its tab.

The three slideshow menus—President, CFO, and Marketing—are still available in the Menu Editor window. These three menus contain the content for an interactive slideshow. The viewer will select buttons on each menu to display the next slide, display the previous slide, or return to the main menu.

You'll use buttons that have already been created for this slideshow. The buttons are layered Photoshop files. Because they are not part of a Photoshop menu, you must import them into the Library palette to retain the layers. If you imported the files as assets, the Photoshop files would be flattened.

5 Choose Window > Library to open the Library palette.

6 Click the Add Item button (⊡) at the bottom of the Library palette.

7 Navigate to the Lesson 10 folder. Select the **Menu_button.psd**, **Next_button.psd**, and **Prev_button.psd** files, and then click Open.

The three buttons have been added to the Library palette.

Laying out a slideshow menu

Add the buttons to one of the menus.

1 In the Library palette, select one of the buttons you just imported. With one of the slideshow menus open in the Menu Editor window, click the Place button at the bottom of the Library palette.

The button you selected appears on the menu.

2 Use the Place button to add the other two buttons to the menu.

3 Click the Show Safe Area button (▣) at the bottom of the Menu Editor window to display the safe area margins.

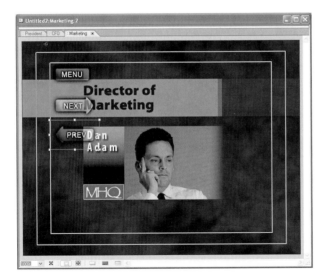

4 Using the selection tool, move the three buttons to the bottom of the menu, within the margins.

The three buttons have different vertical dimensions (that is, they have different heights), so you'll need to align them by their vertical centers.

5 Select all three buttons, and then choose Object > Align > Middle.

Note: The Object > Align > Middle command results in different positioning than the Object > Align > Center command. If you accidentally choose Object > Align > Center, choose Edit > Undo, and then choose Object > Align > Middle.

Now, ensure that the spacing between the buttons is even.

6 With all three buttons selected, choose Object > Distribute > Horizontally.

First, you'll create a link for the Menu button. You'll copy the buttons to the other slideshow menus, and the Menu button will have the same behavior on each menu.

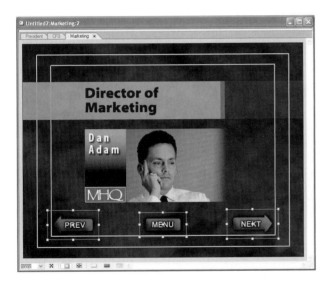

7 Select the Menu button in the Menu Editor window.

8 In the Properties palette, choose Main > Presentation button from the Link pop-up menu.

9 Save the project. Name it **Lesson_10.ncor**

Copying buttons to other menus

In a slideshow, you want the navigational buttons to appear in the same place on each slide. Adobe Encore DVD makes it easy to copy objects in exactly the same location from one menu to another. Copy and paste all three buttons to the other two slideshow menus.

1 Select all three buttons, and choose Edit > Copy.

2 Click the tab for another slideshow menu in the Menu Editor window.

3 Choose Edit > Paste.

The three buttons appear in the same position they occupy in the first slideshow menu.

4 Click the tab for the remaining slideshow menu in the Menu Editor window.

5 Choose Edit > Paste.

Again, the buttons are pasted in the same position.

6 Click on the menu to deselect the buttons. Then select only the Menu button.

In the Properties palette, note that the Menu button has retained its Link setting.

7 Save the project.

Linking menus to each other

The Menu button behaves the same way on each slideshow menu, but the Prev and Next buttons should have different behaviors, depending on the menu. The slideshow menus will appear in this order: President, CFO, Marketing.

1 Click the President tab in the Menu Editor window.

This will be the first slide, so you do not need the Prev button.

2 Select the Prev button with the selection tool, and choose Edit > Clear.

The Prev button has been deleted. The Menu button link is already set, so you need only to set the link for the Next button on this menu.

3 Select the Next button. Then, in the Properties palette, choose CFO > Next Button from the Link pop-up menu.

4 Click the CFO tab in the Menu Editor window.

5 Select the Prev button. Then, in the Properties palette, choose President > Next Button from the Link pop-up menu.

6 Select the Next button, and link it to Marketing > Menu Button.

7 Click the Marketing tab in the Menu Editor window.

This will be the last slide, so you do not need the Next button.

8 Select the Next button with the selection tool, and choose Edit > Clear.

9 Select the Prev button, and link it to CFO > Next Button.

10 In the Project window, double-click the Main menu to open it in the Menu Editor window.

11 Select the Meet the Executive Team button, and link it to President > Next Button.

When the viewer starts the slideshow, the President menu appears first. Preview the slideshow to make sure the links all work as expected.

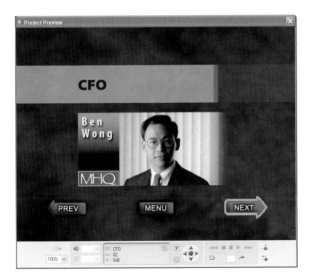

12 Choose File > Preview.

13 Click the Meet the Executive Team button, and then click the navigation buttons you just created to proceed through the slideshow. Be sure to test the Prev and Menu buttons as well as the Next buttons.

14 When you've finished, close the Project Preview window and save the project.

Adding audio to a menu

You'll add an audio track to each menu in the slideshow.

1 Right-click in the Project window, and choose Import as Asset.

2 Navigate to the Lesson 10 folder. Select the **CFO.wav**, **Marketing.wav,** and **President.wav** files, and click Open.

3 Click the President tab in the Menu Editor window, and open the Properties palette.

Notice that Hold Forever is selected next to the Duration field. With the current settings, you need to click on a navigation button to change slides or return to the menu.

4 Drag the President.wav file from the Project window onto the President menu in the Menu Editor window.

5 Click the President menu in the Project window to make it active.

In the Properties palette, notice that the President.wav file is listed in the Audio field, and the duration of the menu has been changed to the duration of the WAV file.

6 Drag the CFO.wav file and the Marketing.wav file onto the CFO and Marketing menus, respectively, in the Menu Editor window.

Previewing an audio file

Now that you've linked the audio files to the menus, preview this portion of the project.

1 In the Project window, right-click the President menu, and choose Preview From Here.

The President menu appears as the audio file plays. When the audio file ends, the screen turns black.

2 Close the Project Preview window.

Obviously, you don't want the screen to turn black, leaving the viewer with no navigation options, when the audio file ends. You can address this in several ways:

• Set the menu to loop. If the audio file were music only, this would be a good option. However, in this project, the voice-over would repeat with each loop and become annoying.

• Set the menu to loop, and set a loop point after the voice-over is done. However, the navigation buttons would not be activated until the loop point is reached.

• Set the end action to link to the next slide.

• Set a longer duration for the slide, and then set an end action with the assumption that the user is not paying attention to the slideshow.

Setting end actions for slideshow menus

The last option appears to be the best option for this project. You'll change the duration and set the end action for all the menus at once.

1 In the Project window, click the Menus tab to display only the menus for this project.

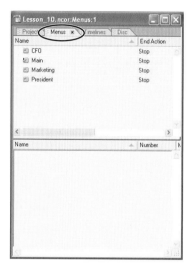

2 Holding down the Ctrl key, select the CFO, Marketing, and President menus in the Project window.

3 In the Properties palette, choose Main > Presentation Button from the End Action pop-up menu in the Properties palette.

If the viewer does not choose a button before the duration ends, the main menu will appear, with the Presentation button highlighted.

4 In the Properties palette, enter 00:01:00:00 for duration.

The viewer will have one minute to make a selection before returning to the main menu.

These behaviors have been set for all of the menus you selected.

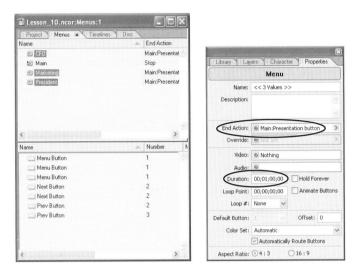

5 Choose File > Preview to test the duration and end action behaviors.

6 Close the Project Preview window.

7 Save the project.

About creating slideshows with timelines

In the first part of this lesson, you created a slideshow using a separate menu for each still image. This method allows the viewer to control the pace of the slideshow—and to return to previous images. However, you must include a separate menu for each image, and you can't include a continuous audio track throughout the slideshow.

If you instead use timelines for slideshows, navigation is more limited, but you have more control over how the slideshow is viewed. You determine the timing of each image, and you can include a continuous audio track (or tracks).

Next, you will re-create a business slideshow presentation. The still images for this part of the lesson were originally created in a presentation software application, and then exported as separate TIFF images. The slides were saved at 720 x 540 pixels (the default). The audio was recorded and imported as a WAV file.

Organizing your assets

In this lesson, you will be using multiple assets. To keep the Project window from getting cluttered, you'll use folders to organize the assets.

1 Click the Project tab in the Project window to make it active, and choose File > New Folder.

2 In the New Folder Name dialog box, type Executive, and click OK.

3 Select all of the assets and menus in the Project window except for the Main menu file, and drag them into the Executive folder.

The Executive folder now holds all the files you used to create the first slideshow.

Note: Folders appear only in the Project tab of the Project window. If you click the Menus or Timelines tab in the Project window, the menus or timelines will display just as if they were all stored together.

4 Right-click in the Project window, and choose New Folder from the context menu.

💡 *You can create a new folder by choosing File > New Folder or by right-clicking in the Project window and choosing New Folder from the context menu. Often there are multiple ways to accomplish a task. Use the method you prefer.*

5 In the New Folder Name dialog box, type **Presentation**, and click OK.

The Presentation folder will hold the assets you'll use to create the second slideshow.

6 Double-click the Presentation folder you just created to open it.

7 Choose File > Import as Asset.

8 Select the **Q2_Earnings.wav** file, and click Open.

The file you imported is added to the Presentation folder in the Project window.

9 Choose File > Import as Asset.

10 Navigate to the Presentation folder in the Lesson 10 folder, and select all of the files in it (**Slide1.tif** through **Slide6.tif**). Then click Open.

11 If it isn't already open, expand the Presentation folder in the Project window by clicking the triangle to the left of it. Note that the files you imported are all in this folder.

Note: If the Presentation folder in the Project window wasn't active when you imported the files, drag them into the Presentation folder now.

12 Save the project.

Creating a timeline from still images

This slideshow will be a single timeline composed of a set of still images exported from a presentation software application. You'll place the images, and then stretch or trim the duration to match the audio of the presentation.

1 Select the Q2_Earnings.wav file in the Project window, and click the Create a New Timeline button at the bottom of the Project window.

A new timeline is created with the WAV file in the Audio 1 track.

First, you will adjust the default duration of all still images in the project.

2 Choose Edit > Preferences > Timelines.

3 Type **8** in the Default Still Length field, and click OK.

By default, each image will remain on the screen for eight seconds.

4 Drag the Slide1.tif file from the Project window to the video track in the timeline.

Slide 1.tif appears in the timeline with a duration of eight seconds. You may need to drag the zoom slider on the Timeline window to the left to display the entire clip.

5 Click the Play button in the Monitor window and listen to the audio track. When the voice says "next slide" (about 06:10), press the Pause button in the Monitor window.

Note: Make sure the audio is on and speakers or a headphone are attached to your computer.

6 Put the cursor over the right edge of the Slide1.tif clip. When the cursor turns into a double-sided arrow, click and drag the edge to the current-time indicator.

You've shortened the slide so that the next slide will appear when you hear "next slide" in the audio.

7 Drag Slide2.tif to the video track, just to the right of the Slide1.tif clip.

8 Click the Play button in the Monitor window, and listen to the audio track again. When you hear "next slide" again (about 21:27), press the Pause button in the Monitor window.

9 Again, put the cursor over the right edge of the Slide2.tif clip, and when the cursor turns into a double-sided arrow, click and drag the edge to the current-time indicator.

You've lengthened the time that the slide is displayed so that the screen does not go black before the next slide.

Notice that a chapter point has been placed in the timeline where the slides change. You can use these chapter points for simple navigation when playing the DVD by clicking the Next or Previous buttons on the remote control.

10 Repeat steps 7-9 for Slide3.tif, Slide4.tif, Slide5.tif, and Slide6.tif. The slide transitions will be at approximately 30 seconds, 44 seconds, and 53 seconds. (For this project, you don't need to be precise.)

11 Trim the last clip (Slide6.tif) to the end of the audio track.

If you want all slides to have the same exact duration, set the duration in Preferences, create a new timeline, and then drag all the slides to the video track at once. The slides will appear in alphanumeric order in a single timeline. It is important to create the timeline first. If, instead, you select all of the slides and then create a new timeline, each slide will be placed into its own timeline.

12 In the Project window, right-click the Q2_earnings timeline (not Q2_earnings.wav), and choose Preview From Here.

13 Watch to make sure that the slide changes are appropriate for the audio track. In the Project Preview window, the audio may skip slightly at the transition points, but the final disc should not have this problem.

14 Close the Project Preview window, and save the project.

Setting behaviors for a slideshow

The timeline is created. Now you just need to set the behaviors for it.

1 In the Project window, select the Q2_earnings timeline.

2 In the Properties palette, choose Main > Meet Button from the End Action pop-up menu. Choose Main > Meet Button from the Menu Remote pop-up menu.

If you want to create a looping, self-running slideshow, set the end action of the timeline to the first chapter point of the same timeline.

3 In the Project window, click the Menus tab. Select the Main menu in the Menus tab.

4 Click the Presentation button in the lower pane of the Menus tab.

5 In the Properties palette, choose Q2_earnings > Chapter 1 from the Link pop-up menu.

Previewing the project

Verify that the links behave as you expect them to.

1 Choose File > Preview.

2 Verify that each button links to the appropriate timeline or menu, and that the end actions are appropriate.

3 Save the project.

Burning the DVD

Burn the DVD using the Build DVD command.

1 Choose File > Build DVD > Make DVD Disc.

2 Choose Current Project from the Create Using pop-up menu, and specify your DVD recorder.

3 Insert a blank disc, and click Next.

Review questions

1 What are the advantages and disadvantages to creating a slideshow from menus?

2 What are the advantages and disadvantages to creating a slideshow from a timeline?

3 How can you ensure that buttons are in the same place on multiple menus?

4 How can you specify how long a menu stays on the screen?

5 How can you organize assets in the Project window?

Review answers

1 A slideshow composed of menus gives the viewer greater control over navigation and the timing of each transition. However, it can be cumbersome to create individual menus for a slideshow that includes numerous images, and you do not have control over the way the slideshow is viewed. Additionally, you cannot include an audio track that will play continuously throughout the slideshow.

2 You control exactly how the slideshow is viewed when you create it as a timeline, and you can add an audio track that plays continuously. However, viewers have less control over the navigation and timing.

3 Position the buttons on one menu, and then select them all and copy them. Paste them onto other menus. Adobe Encore DVD pastes them in the same position they occupied in the original menu.

4 To specify how long a menu stays on the screen, select the menu in the Project window and then specify a Duration value in the Properties palette.

5 You can create folders to organize assets for a complex project in the Project window. To create a folder, choose File > New Folder. Then drag existing assets into the folder, or select the folder before importing assets to add them to the folder automatically.

Lesson 11

11 | Adding Audio Tracks and Subtitles

Many DVD projects are designed for more than one audience. You can add audio tracks and subtitle tracks for different languages, accessible through menus you create in Adobe Encore DVD.

In previous lessons, you've worked primarily with menus, links, and behaviors. In this lesson, you'll focus on timelines. Using Adobe Encore DVD, you can add up to 8 audio tracks and 32 subtitle tracks to your DVD. Most DVD players can play only one audio track and one subtitle track at a time, but offering multiple tracks gives your audience more options and lets you reach more people. In this lesson you will learn how to do the following:

- Add an audio track to a timeline.
- Assign a language to an audio track.
- Designate the active audio track.
- Link buttons to audio tracks.
- Add subtitle tracks to a timeline.
- Type subtitles directly onto the Monitor window.
- Import subtitles from a text script.
- Assign a language to a subtitle track.
- Change the duration or timing of a subtitle.
- Link buttons to subtitles.

Getting started

In this lesson, you'll add audio files and subtitle tracks to a timeline, using audio, graphic, and video files included on the *Adobe Encore DVD Classroom in a Book* DVD. Make sure you know the location of the files you need for Lesson 11. For help, see "Copying the Classroom in a Book files" on page 2.

Make sure audio is enabled on your computer, and that headphones or speakers are plugged in, so that you can hear the audio files you'll be working with.

Viewing the finished Adobe Encore DVD project

To see what you'll be creating, take a look at the finished project.

1 Start Adobe Encore DVD.

2 Choose File > Open Project.

3 In the Open dialog box, navigate to the Lesson 11 folder. Select **Lesson_11_end.ncor,** and then click Open.

4 Choose File > Preview.

The Project Preview window opens, and a menu appears. The menu has two buttons.

5 Click the Languages button. Click the two language buttons in the menu to play the same video with different language voice-overs. Click the Back button to return to the main menu.

6 Click the Subtitles button.

7 Click the two buttons in the menu to play the same video with and without English subtitles.

8 Close the Project Preview window and the Lesson_11_end Project window.

Including audio tracks in a project

Audio tracks can provide a mood for your video, enhance understanding, or simply make the video more appealing. You can use music tracks, voice-overs, natural sounds, or any other sounds that can be captured on audiotape. In this section, you'll add two different language tracks for a single video track. The viewer will then be able to choose a language.

First, import the assets.

1 In Adobe Encore DVD, choose File > New Project. Click OK to accept NTSC as the television standard.

2 Choose File > Import as Asset. Navigate to the Lesson 11 folder. Select the **English.wav** and **Rose.avi** files. Click Open.

The Rose.avi file includes an audio soundtrack with a Dutch voice-over. The English.wav file is an audio file that contains a voice-over in English.

3 Choose File > Import as Menu. Navigate to the Lesson 11 folder. Select the **Language.psd** file. Click Open.

This menu offers the viewer a choice between language soundtracks.

💡 *You can play only one audio track at a time. If you want to play music with a voice-over, for example, or a director's comments over the regular soundtrack, you'll need to mix two audio tracks in another application, such as Adobe Premiere Pro or Adobe Audition™, and then save the file as a single audio track to use in Adobe Encore DVD.*

Adding audio tracks

When you create the timeline for the Rose.avi file, its audio track will also appear in the timeline. You'll add an audio track for the English.wav file you imported.

1 In the Project window, select the Rose.avi file, and then choose Timeline > New Timeline.

A new timeline is created for the video and audio tracks in the Rose.avi file, and the Monitor window opens.

2 Click the Play button in the Monitor window.

The video plays, and a voice gives a commentary in Dutch.

3 Choose nl-Dutch from the pop-up menu to the right of the Audio 1 name in the Timeline window.

Adobe Encore DVD recognizes the audio track as Dutch. Now add the other audio track.

4 Choose Timeline > Add Audio Track.

A new track appears in the Timeline window, with the name Audio 2.

5 Drag the English.wav file from the Project window onto the Audio 2 track in the Timeline window.

The English.wav file appears in the audio track. The speaker icon (🔊) to the left of Audio 2 indicates that Audio 2 is the active audio track. Only one audio track can be active at a time.

6 Choose en-English from the pop-up menu to the right of the Audio 2 name in the timeline.

7 Click the Play button in the Monitor window again.

The soundtrack is in English, because the English.wav file is the active audio track. To make the Dutch audio track active, click the box next to Audio 1 so that the speaker icon appears.

8 Save the project as **Lesson_11.ncor**.

Previewing audio tracks

You can preview both of the audio tracks while watching the video clip.

1 In the Project window, right-click the Rose timeline, and choose Preview From Here.

The Project Preview window opens and plays the Rose timeline, even though it isn't set as first play. Use the Preview From Here command to begin previewing your project exactly where you want to, without having to navigate through menus.

The first audio track plays. In this case, it's the Dutch soundtrack.

2 In the Project Preview window, click the Mute Audio button (◀)) to toggle audio on and off.

3 Choose 2 en from the pop-up menu next to the Mute Audio button.

The audio changes to English.

4 Close the Project Preview window.

Linking buttons to audio tracks

You've added the audio tracks. Now you will link the buttons in the Language menu to them.

1 Open the Language menu in the Menu Editor window, if it isn't already open.

2 With the selection tool, right-click the Dutch button in the menu, and choose Link To. The Specify Link dialog box appears.

3 Select the Rose timeline. Then choose 1 from the Audio pop-up menu at the bottom of the dialog box. Choose Off from the Subtitles pop-up menu. Click OK.

When the viewer activates the Dutch button, the first soundtrack will play with the video. You'll be adding a subtitle track later, but you don't want it to appear when the viewer activates the Dutch button in the Language menu; choosing Off ensures that no subtitles will appear.

4 With the selection tool, right-click the English button in the menu, and choose Link To.

The Specify Link dialog box appears.

5 Select the Rose timeline. Then choose 2 from the Audio pop-up menu at the bottom of the dialog box, and click OK.

When the viewer activates the English button, the Rose timeline will play with the second soundtrack.

6 In the Project window, select the Rose timeline.

7 In the Properties palette, choose Language > Dutch from the End Action pop-up menu.

When the video finishes, the Language menu reappears, with the Dutch button highlighted.

8 Choose Language > Dutch from the Menu Remote pop-up menu.

When a viewer presses the Menu button on a remote control while the video is playing, the Language menu will appear, with the Dutch button highlighted.

9 Save the project. Name it **Lesson_11.ncor.**

Adding a main menu

In this project, viewers can choose either a soundtrack language or a language for subtitles. You'll add a main menu to help viewers navigate to the Language menu, and to define the behaviors between the main menu and the Language menu.

1 Choose File > Import as Menu and select **Roses_main.psd**.

2 In the Menu Editor window, select the Languages button in the Roses_main menu.

3 In the Properties palette, choose Language > Dutch from the Link pop-up menu.

When the viewer activates the Languages button, the Language menu will appear, with the Dutch button highlighted.

4 Click the Language tab in the Menu Editor window.

5 Select the Back button in the Language menu and then, in the Properties palette, choose Roses_main > Subtitles from the Link pop-up menu.

When the viewer activates the Back button, the Roses_main menu will appear, with the Subtitles button highlighted.

6 In the Project window, right-click the Roses_main menu, and choose Set as First Play.

When the DVD is inserted into the player, the Roses_main menu will appear on the screen.

7 Choose File > Preview.

8 Click the Languages button, and then click the Dutch or English button.

The appropriate audio track should play. Notice that the field next to the Mute Audio button displays the track number and language code you specified (nl or en).

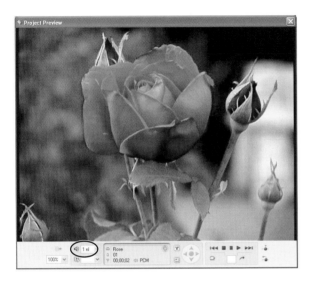

9 Click the other language button.

The correct language should play, and the Language menu should appear after the timeline is done.

10 Close the Project Preview window.

11 Save the project.

Adding a subtitle track

Subtitles are words that appear on the screen. You can use subtitles to enable viewers to follow dialogue, even when they are hearing-impaired or do not speak the language used in the audio soundtrack. Or you can use subtitles to emphasize points made in the audio soundtrack. In this project, you'll create an English subtitle track to accompany the video.

First, you'll add the English subtitle track. One way to add subtitles is to type directly onto the Monitor window.

1 Click the Rose timeline to ensure that it is active.

2 Choose Timeline > Add Subtitle Track.

A new track titled Subtitle 1 appears under the Audio tracks.

3 Choose en-English from the pop-up menu next to the Subtitle 1 name in the Timeline window.

4 Move the current-time indicator to the beginning of the timeline.

5 Click the Play button in the Monitor window, and click the Pause button when the voice-over begins.

Note: If the Monitor window isn't open, choose Window > Monitor.

6 Move the current-time indicator to the point in the timeline where the voice-over begins (about 01:20).

7 With the text tool, click an insertion point in the lower part of the video in the Monitor window.

8 Choose Window > Character to open the Character palette.

9 Choose Myriad Pro for the font, Regular for the font style, and 40 for the type size. Click the Align Center option.

10 Type **This is one of the most classic** and then press Enter.

11 Type **roses that I have developed.**

The text appears over the video.

12 Press the Ctrl button. The cursor turns into an arrow (▶). Drag the text block so that it is centered in the frame.

A bar appears in the Subtitle 1 track in the Timeline window. The text you typed in the Monitor window displays in the bar. The bar does not go to the end of the timeline, but it covers a few seconds of time.

13 Move the current-time indicator to 00:00. Click the Play button in the Monitor window.

The subtitle appears onscreen as the first voice-over sentence plays, and disappears after a few seconds.

14 Save the project.

Modifying the appearance of subtitles

You can change the color of the subtitles to ensure that they are visible as the colors of the video change. You can also alter the timing and duration of a subtitle after you've created it.

1 Move the current-time indicator to a point past the first subtitle bar (about 06:00).

2 In the Monitor window, use the text tool to type **It has deep pink blooms** and then press Enter.

3 Type **and a strong fragrance.**

4 In the Monitor window, use the selection tool to position the subtitle text block.

5 In the Properties palette, choose Group 2 from the Color Group pop-up menu, and then choose Group 3.

The color of the subtitle changes. If the subtitle blends in with the video image, you can change the color to enhance the legibility. If further color changes are needed, you can choose Edit > Color Sets > Timeline and edit the colors.

6 Reposition the second bar in the Subtitle 1 track by dragging it to the right, so that it begins at about 06:15.

After you create it, you can move the subtitle to appear at a different point in the video.

7 Place the cursor over the left edge of the subtitle bar. When the cursor turns to a double-sided arrow, drag the edge of the bar to the 06:00 point.

You've changed the in point of the subtitle, so it will appear on screen longer. You can change the out point the same way: place the cursor over the right edge until it becomes a double-sided arrow, and then drag it to the new out point.

8 In the Project window, right-click the Rose timeline, and choose Preview From Here.

9 As the timeline plays in the Project Preview window, click the Toggle Subtitle Display button (⬚) (directly under the Mute Audio button) to turn the subtitles on and off.

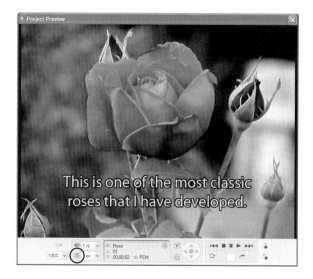

10 Close the Project Preview window.

11 Select the bars in the Subtitle 1 track, and choose Edit > Clear. The subtitles you typed are deleted.

12 Save the project.

Importing subtitles from a text script

You typed subtitles directly onto the Monitor window, but typing subtitles can become tedious for a long or complex video. It's often more efficient to import the subtitles from a text file.

1 Click the Rose timeline to make it active, and then choose Timeline > Import Subtitles > Text Script.

2 In the Open dialog box, select **English_subtitles.txt**, and click Open.

3 In the Import Subtitles (Text Script) dialog box, choose Myriad Pro for the font, Regular for the font style, and 40 for the type size. Click the Align Center option.

4 In the Subtitle Settings section of the dialog box, choose 1 and en-English from the Track pop-up menus. Click OK.

This dialog box displays a preview, including the safe area margins. When you click OK, Adobe Encore DVD places the subtitles in the Subtitle 1 track. Look at the Timeline window to see how the subtitles are distributed.

5 Click the Play button in the Monitor window.

Note: If the Monitor window isn't open, choose Window > Monitor.

The video plays, and the subtitles appear on screen. There is a misspelled word in the third subtitle. You'll need to edit it.

6 Move the current-time indicator to 12:00.

The subtitle you need to edit appears on the screen.

7 With the text tool, change the word **Ths** to **This**. Then select the selection tool to deselect the text tool, and click outside the text block in the Monitor window.

You can edit the subtitles that you import as a text script. You can also change the timing and duration of the subtitles.

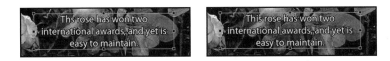

Note: Changes you make to the imported subtitles do not affect the original text file you imported.

8 Save the project.

About subtitle scripts

You can import subtitles into Adobe Encore DVD if you have prepared them in a text file first. A subtitle script includes a separate line for each subtitle. Each line is composed of the initial timecode (the time at which the subtitle is to appear), the final timecode (the time at which the subtitle is to disappear), and the subtitle text itself. To see a subtitle script from which you can model your own, open the English_subtitles.txt file in the Lesson11 folder in a text editor, such as Windows Notepad.

Linking buttons to subtitle tracks

Now you'll link the subtitle tracks to a menu, so that your viewers can choose whether to view subtitles or not.

1 Click in the Project window and then choose File > Import as Menu, and import the **Subtitle.psd** file.

2 With the selection tool, right-click the Dutch button in the Menu Editor window, and choose Link To.

The Specify Link dialog box appears.

3 Select the Rose timeline. Choose 1 from the Audio pop-up menu and Off from the Subtitle pop-up menu. Click OK.

When the viewer activates the Dutch button, the video will play with the Dutch soundtrack and no subtitles will appear on the screen.

```
Target:  Rose:Chapter 1

Audio:  1        v      Subtitle:  Off       v
```

4 Right-click the English Subtitles button, and choose Link To.

5 Select Rose. Choose 1 from the Audio pop-up menu and 1 from the Subtitle pop-up menu, and then click OK.

When the viewer activates the English Subtitles button, the video will play with the Dutch soundtrack and English subtitles.

```
Target:  Rose:Chapter 1

Audio:  1        v      Subtitle:  1        v
```

6 Hold down the Shift key as you select both buttons in the Menu Editor window.

7 In the Properties palette, choose Subtitle > Dutch from the Override pop-up menu.

Earlier you set the end action for the timeline to return to the Language menu. Because you set this override, when viewers play the video using one of these buttons, they'll return to the Subtitles menu after it finishes.

```
 Library   Layers   Character   Properties

                  Button

      Name:  << 2 Values >>
    Number:                v
  Highlight:               v

      Link:  ● Rose:Chapter 1        A1 S-  >
  Override:  ● Subtitle :Dutch              >

           □ Auto Activate
           □ Create Text Subpicture
```

8 Select the Back button in the Subtitles menu.

9 In the Properties palette, choose Roses_main > Languages from the Link pop-up menu.

Note: If you don't see the Roses_main option in the pop-up menu, double-click the Roses_main menu in the Project window to open it in the Menu Editor window.

10 Click the Roses_main tab in the Menu Editor window.

11 Select the Subtitles button.

12 In the Properties palette, choose Subtitle > Dutch from the Link pop-up menu.

13 Save the project.

Previewing the project

Verify that the project behaves as you expect it to before burning it to disc.

1 Choose File > Preview.

2 Click the buttons to navigate through the menus. Verify that the audio and subtitle tracks play when they should.

3 Close the Project Preview window when you're done.

Note: If the subtitles don't display in the Preview window, make sure the Toggle Subtitle Display button at the bottom of the Preview window is selected.

Burning a DVD

Burn the DVD using the Build DVD command.

1 Choose File > Build DVD > Make DVD Disc.

2 Choose Current Project from the Create Using pop-up menu, and specify your DVD recorder.

Insert a blank disc, and click Next.

Review questions

1 How do you add an audio track to a timeline?

2 How do you assign a language to an audio track?

3 How many audio tracks can play at one time?

4 Name two ways to add subtitle text to a video.

5 How can you change the duration of a subtitle, so that it appears on screen longer?

Review answers

1 Select the timeline, and then choose Timeline > Add Audio Track. Drag the audio file onto the new audio track.

2 Choose the language from the pop-up menu next to the name of the audio track in the Timeline window.

3 Only one audio track can play at a time. If you want to play both music and a voice-over, for example, merge the audio files in an audio-editing application before you import the file into Adobe Encore DVD.

4 You can type directly onto the Monitor window with the text tool, or import a text script.

5 Place the cursor over the end of the bar in the subtitle track until it becomes a double-sided arrow, and then drag it to the new in or out point in the timeline.

Index